PICKLEBALL BASICS: THE ESSENTIAL GUIDE FOR EVERY FAMILY

EFFORTLESSLY DIVE INTO PLAY AND BOND EVEN IF YOU'VE NEVER HELD A PADDLE BEFORE

JAMES STUART

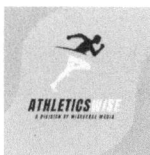

Published by AthleticsWISE, a division of WISEVerse Media LLC, Sarasota, Florida, United States of America

First edition

ISBN 979-8-9893317-5-8 (paperback)
ISBN 979-8-9893317-6-5 (hardcover)

CONTENTS

PREFACE

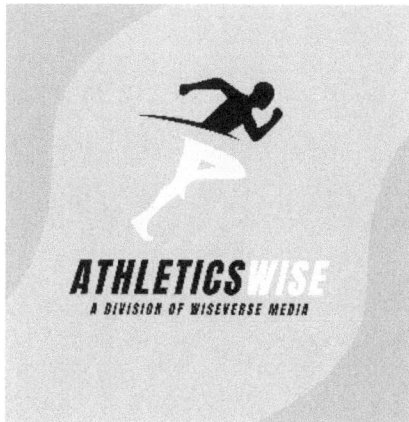

ATHLETICSWISE
A DIVISION OF WISEVERSE MEDIA

Written by an avid pickleball family, " *Pickleball Basics: The Essential Guide for Every Family* isn't just a book; it's an experience – a journey crafted to bond families and ignite a shared passion. Designed with every family member in mind, each page is infused with humor, engaging anecdotes, and a sprinkle of pickleball trivia that is as entertaining as the game itself.

This book is designed to be read with your kids, or by yourself, sharing jokes and anecdotes along the way. Even better, listen to the audiobook version in the car and experience the jokes and trivia together all the while piquing your family's interest in pickleball.

Published by AthleticsWISE
a division of WISEVerse Media

INTRODUCTION

WHY PICKLEBALL? THE STUART FAMILY'S JOURNEY TO DISCOVERING PICKLEBALL

It was an ordinary Sunday morning, with the sun's rays casting a warm glow over the Stuart household. The scent of pancakes wafted through the air as the kids, Isaac and Ellie, wrestled in the living room. Their parents, Jane and James, busied themselves in the kitchen.

Amid the morning ruckus, Jane's phone chimed with a message. It was from her energetic colleague, Lucy. "Ever tried pickleball?" the message read, followed by an invitation to the local court that afternoon. Jane, intrigued, called the family to breakfast and announced, "We're trying something new today: pickleball."

James raised an eyebrow. "Is that some kind of game where you toss pickles?"

Ellie's face contorted in disgust. "Ew! No, thanks!" Isaac, however, jumped at the prospect of a new adventure. "Could be fun! Let's give it a shot."

After breakfast, Jane pulled out her phone to search for the rules. It turned out pickleball was a mix of tennis, badminton, and table tennis. The equipment required was minimal: a solid paddle and a perforated ball. They could easily rent the equipment from the court.

The Stuarts soon found themselves at the local community center. The pickleball court was buzzing with activity. There was an intoxicating rhythm of paddles hitting balls, laughter, and players darting back and forth.

Lucy greeted them with her usual radiant smile and enthusiasm, "Welcome to pickleball paradise!" Handing them paddles and balls, she gave a brief rundown of the rules.

Paired up for a friendly match, Jane and James faced off against Isaac and Ellie. As beginners, their serves mostly went astray, and there were many double bounces. But with every missed shot, the family laughed harder.

Ellie, who usually despised sports, found herself genuinely enjoying the game—much to everyone's surprise. Isaac, on the other hand, emerged as the anticipated star. His swift reflexes and keen eye had him placing shots expertly, leaving his parents scrambling. Every missed ball from other players was met with his dramatic cry of "Noooo!" sending everyone into peals of laughter.

In the middle of their game, an older couple approached them. With a twinkle in their eyes, they challenged the Stuarts to a friendly match. Their names were Alan and Molly, seasoned pickleball players.

Jane hesitated. "We're just beginners. I doubt we'd be a good match for you."

Molly winked. "Don't worry, dear. We'll go easy on you."

What transpired next was nothing short of a pickleball masterclass. Alan and Molly, with their synchronized moves and tactical placements, had the Stuarts dashing and diving, often in the wrong directions.

However, the older couple's skills didn't dampen the Stuarts' spirits. In fact, they cheered for every point the couple scored against them, taking the game in stride and relishing the learning experience.

When the match ended, and Alan and Molly emerged victorious, the Stuarts were all smiles and out of breath. As they sat down to rest, James exclaimed, "That was intense and so much fun!"

Jane nodded in agreement. "It's a great way to bond. I can't remember the last time we laughed so much."

Isaac was already planning the next outing. "We need to practice and challenge George and Martha again. We need a rematch!"

Ellie chimed in, "But first, we need our own paddles. Customized!"

Lucy, overhearing them, laughed. "Welcome to the world of pickleball. You're officially hooked."

As the sun set and the courts started emptying, the Stuarts headed home, muscles sore but hearts full. The day had not only introduced them to a new sport but had also woven new memories of laughter, camaraderie, and playful competitiveness.

That night, as Jane tucked Ellie into bed, Ellie whispered, "Mom, pickleball's way cooler than throwing pickles. Can we play again next weekend?"

Jane kissed her forehead. "Definitely."

And thus, the Stuarts' love affair with pickleball began, a sport that brought them closer than ever. Within days, they were back, paddles in hand, ready to embark on their pickleball journey.

But why pickleball ... you might wonder? Well, ask the Stuarts, and they'll talk about the unique blend of energy, strategy, and camaraderie that the game brought. But there's something more universal here, beyond the four walls of the Stuart residence. Across towns, cities, and countries, pickleball has been sweeping hearts and minds. It's not just about the exhilarating matches; it's about the human connections formed, the rivalries developed, and the personal growth witnessed.

You see, bonding through sports isn't a new concept. From the ancient Olympic Games to backyard football matches, sports have always brought people together, bridging gaps and fostering community. But pickleball? It's a newer kid on the block with a quirky name to boot. Yet, its rapid rise in popularity tells a tale. The game offers something refreshing, accessible, and infectious in its allure.

This book is your golden ticket to that world. A world where the racket's swing becomes a dance move, where each serve is a promise of a challenge, and where every match, whether won or lost, leaves you craving for more. We'll gear up together, learn the rules, decode strategies, and even stumble on a few hurdles. But through it all, you'll find stories like the Stuarts'— stories of love, laughter, and life lessons—both on and off the court.

So, whether you're an Isaac, eager and ready to jump in, or an Ellie, skeptical but willing to give it a shot, there's a place for you in this pickleball journey. Buckle up, for we're about to serve up a tale that's more than just about a game. It's about a community, a passion, and the magic that happens when the two collide.

ELLIE   ISAAC

WHAT'S INSIDE?

1. **Get to Know Pickleball:** Journey through time to discover the roots of this intriguing game and explore why it's caught on like wildfire.

2. **Gearing Up – Equipment Essentials:** Get the lowdown on the must-have tools of the trade, from paddles to balls and everything in between.

3. **Grasping the Ground Rules:** Unravel the rules that govern the game and become a pickleball pro in no time.

4. **Strategies for Success:** Unlock the secrets to mastering the court and making every move count.

5. **Practice Makes Perfect:** Unearth effective drills and practice routines to hone your skills.

6. **Common Hurdles and How to Jump over Them:**

Tackle those pesky challenges head-on and turn them into learning experiences.

7. **Beyond the Court – Life Lessons from Pickleball:** Reflect on the life-changing insights this sport has to offer, both within and beyond the court boundaries.

8. **Joining the Pickleball Community:** Navigate the vibrant and welcoming world of pickleball enthusiasts and find your place among them.

9. **Etiquette and Fair Play:** Embrace the unwritten rules of respect, courtesy, and sportsmanship that define the game's spirit.

10. **Venturing into Competitive Play:** Take your game to the next level and experience the thrill of competitive pickleball.

11. **And more ...**

And to make this fun, you'll find loads of fun facts and jokes along the way.

CHAPTER 1

THE HISTORY & APPEAL OF PICKLEBALL

Welcome to the world of pickleball! In this first chapter, we'll cover all the fundamentals you need to know to get started with this fun, friendly game.

DID YOU KNOW?

Pickleball is a combination of badminton, tennis, and table tennis.

HISTORY OF PICKLEBALL

Tracing back its roots, pickleball wasn't the result of a grand vision but rather a product of ingenuity and spontaneity. In the summer of 1965, on Bainbridge Island near Seattle, three dads —Joel Pritchard, Bill Bell, and Barney McCallum—wanted to entertain their bored kids. Finding their badminton equipment missing, they improvised with ping-pong paddles and a perforated ball. What are the game's dimensions? Borrowed from badminton. Thus, pickleball was born, and the kids? Bored no more. As they refined the game, they realized that the smaller court size and slower pace made it accessible to people of all ages, making it particularly popular among families and older individuals. The sport quickly gained popularity on Bainbridge Island and the surrounding areas. Over the years, the sport evolved from these makeshift beginnings to a structured game with official rules, tournaments, and a growing fanbase.

WHAT'S IN A NAME?

Now, you might be wondering how the game ended up with such a peculiar name. Did it involve pickles? Was it possible that the first ball bore a resemblance to a pickle, giving the game its name? Well, the tale is even quirkier! It's a game named after a dog's fascination with a ball. Sounds like the kind of bizarre factoid that pops up in a late-night trivia game, doesn't it? Well, rumor has it that pickleball owes its peculiar moniker to just such a story. Some believe it was christened "pickleball" because of "Pickles," a cocker spaniel who belonged to one of the co-founders. This playful pup had a penchant for chasing after the perforated balls used in the game. Whether it's a true origin or just a colorful tale, the name adds to the unique charm of this sport.

WHY IS PICKLEBALL GROWING IN POPULARITY?

Now, you might wonder, "Why the growing fuss over a game born from a mishmash of sports?" Well, pickleball's appeal is multifaceted. The learning curve? Quite gentle. Unlike many sports that require weeks or even months to grasp, pickleball's basics can be picked up in a day. Then there's the affordability factor. You don't need to break the bank to start playing—a basic paddle and ball, and you're in the game. And let's not forget its universality. Whether you're 8 or 80, pickleball's allure transcends age. Grandparents can face off against their grand-kids, leveling the playing field in delightful ways.

For a game that was the result of a happy accident, pickleball has come a long way. From the backyards of Bainbridge Island, it quickly spread to the backyards of neighbors, then to local schools, and before anyone knew it, it was the talk of the town!

The first official pickleball tournament was held in 1976 in Tukwila, Washington. From there, the sport's popularity grew even more. In 2005, the USA Pickleball Association (USAPA) was founded to help organize the sport and establish official rules. With the formation of the USAPA, pickleball has grown from a backyard pastime to a nationally recognized sport.

Pickleball has been the fastest-growing sport in America for the last three years, growing at a staggering rate of 158.6% during this time, with an estimated 8.9M players in the US in 2022.[1] Players 18–34 years of age make up the largest number of pickleball players nationwide, at roughly 29%, a significant change in recent years from its initial perception as a sport for retirees.[1] Pickleball player growth was the fastest among players under 24 years of age, at roughly 21%.[1]

Why was the pickleball court so hot? Because all the fans left early!

HA HA HA

In short, pickleball is rapidly growing, and not just in the US. Pickleball is also growing worldwide, as evidenced by the formation of the International Pickleball Federation (IPF), formerly known as the International Foundation of Pickleball, which began organizing international play in 2010. The IPF has extended its reach to encompass over 80 member nations, with that number continually increasing. As more countries affiliate with the IPF, the collective aspiration of introducing pickleball to the Olympic stage becomes ever closer to realization.[2]

WHY FAMILIES LOVE PICKLEBALL

This sport was established on the principle of spending time with family and fostering community connections. Weekend outings to the local courts have become a ritual for many. And why? For starters, there's the undeniable community spirit. Entire families and groups can participate, fostering connections with fellow players and nurturing a sense of belonging. The physical benefits are a major plus too. It's an excellent way to stay active, improve hand-eye coordination, and enhance cardiovascular health. But the cherry on top? The cognitive advantages. For kids, the sport fosters strategic thinking and concentration. For seniors, it aids in keeping the mind sharp, offering a fun alternative to mundane memory exercises.

The magnetism of pickleball, thus, isn't a fluke. It's a testament to how a simple game, born from the need to kill summertime blues, can grow into a tradition embraced by families across generations.

Pickleball is the fastest growing sport in the America with an estimated 8.9m players in 2022.[1]

Before you go further, check out this hilarious video by the
Holderness Family on the 5 Stages of Pickleball.[3] See you in the
obsession stage soon!

WOULD YOU RATHER?

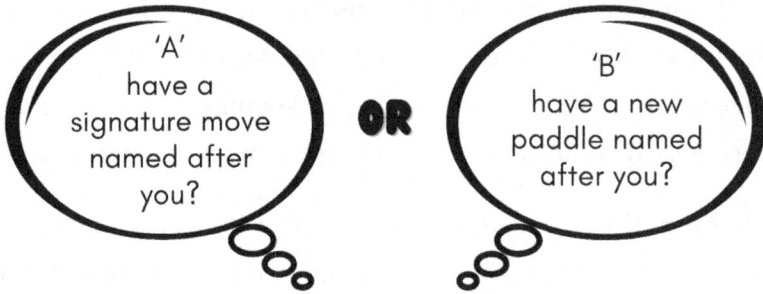

'A'
have a
signature move
named after
you?

OR

'B'
have a new
paddle named
after you?

BENEFITS FOR FAMILIES

Now that you've learned a little more about the sport, the
benefits of pickleball for people and families of all ages should
become more and more evident. For starters, they include:

- Promotes Family Bonding – Pickleball is a great shared activity that brings family members together through cooperative gameplay and quality time. Playing together fosters communication, teamwork, and stronger relationships.
- Fun Exercise for All Ages – Pickleball provides a fun way for family members of all generations to get active exercise. The game gets the heart pumping and engages muscles without high impact.
- Develops and Maintains Hand-Eye Coordination – The paddle and ball skills of pickleball help develop and improve hand-eye coordination in kids and adults.
- Teaches Life Lessons – Valuable lessons like patience, good sportsmanship, self-control, and perseverance can all be learned through family pickleball.
- Creates Shared Memories – The laughs, thrills, and accomplishments.

Can't get your kids interested? Show them the Boys Under 14[4] and Girls Under 14[5] gold medal match from the 2023 Juniors US Pickleball Open and let them see real kids just like them having fun and competing. Then show them this fun video of one family's pickleball battel – losers do the chores![6] They can have fun and play at any level that interests them.

In the next chapter, we'll delve deeper into the equipment essentials, ensuring that whether you're a seasoned player or a newbie, you're always game ready. After all, in a sport named after a ball-chasing dog, you'd want to be armed with the best! [7]

CELEBRITY
spotlight

Bill Gates

HE'S KIND OF A BIG DILL: BILL GATES HAS BEEN A "PICKLER" FOR MORE THAN 50 YEARS. IN FACT, HIS FATHER WAS FRIENDS WITH PICKLEBALL INVENTORS – JOEL PRITCHARD, BILL BELL, AND BARNEY MCCALLUM – LEADING HIS DAD TO BUILD A COURT AT THEIR HOME IN THE LATE 1960S, AND BILL HAS PLAYED THE GAME CONTINUOUSLY EVER SINCE.[7]

CHAPTER 2
GEARING UP –
EQUIPMENT ESSENTIALS

If there's one thing that pickleballers love as much as the game itself, it's their gear. From paddles to balls, there's a whole world of pickleball paraphernalia out there. And while it's not about the gear, having the right equipment and knowing how to use it can definitely give you a leg up—in this case, a paddle up.

Imagine walking into a bustling sports store with your family on the hunt for the perfect pickleball paddle. It's akin to that moment in "Harry Potter" when a young wizard is choosing their first wand. There's a murmur of excitement, a hint of uncertainty. The youngest, eyes wide with curiosity, picks up a flashy paddle and asks, "Is this the one? Will this make me the LeBron of pickleball?" The eldest, perhaps more discerning, examines paddles like a detective—feeling the grip, testing the weight, and judging the aesthetics.

And so, we find ourselves at the very heart of the pickleball gear universe—the paddle. This humble piece of equipment is your sword on the court, your partner in crime, and your magic wand that can turn a ball into a winning shot. But before you rush out to buy the shiniest paddle on the shelf, let's talk about what makes a great pickleball paddle.

PICKING THE PERFECT PADDLE

Paddle Material

The pickleball paddle is one of the most important pieces of equipment. The world of pickleball paddles isn't one-size-fits-all. There are several types to choose from, starting with one of three types of materials.

1. **Wooden paddles** are the OGs (originals) of the paddle world. These are the classics, akin to the original Super Mario games. They might lack some modern features but deliver on that genuine, old-school feel.

2. **Composite paddles** are made of a blend of materials, often featuring a core of polymer, Nomex, or aluminum. Imagine the "Avengers" team—a blend of unique superheroes (materials) coming together to create a force to be reckoned with. A composite paddle brings together the best of materials, providing balance and versatility.

3. **Graphite paddles** are lightweight and agile, perfect for those fast reaction plays. Light as a feather, yet as

responsive as Spider-Man's spidey senses. These paddles are perfect for those with a penchant for speed and finesse.

Price vs. Quality

Materials play a pivotal role in performance, and you get what you pay for, which leads to the age-old debate: **Price vs. Quality.** Investing in a pricier paddle can be a game-changer. Think of it as choosing between a generic cola and a classic Coke. Both serve the same purpose, but one just hits differently. The cost of pickleball paddles can vary significantly based on the brand, material, and specific features of the paddle. With that said, here's a general price range:

- **Entry-level paddles:** These typically range from $20 to $50. They are often made of wood or less expensive composite materials. They're great for beginners who are just trying out the sport.
- **Mid-range paddles:** These paddles usually cost between $50 to $100. They are commonly made from composite or graphite materials, offering a better feel and more advanced features than the entry-level paddles.
- **High-end paddles:** These paddles can range from $100 to $200 (or even more for custom or premium models). They offer the best materials, typically graphite or advanced composites, and are often preferred by advanced or professional players due to their performance features.

For casual backyard fun, the budget-friendly options might just do the trick. For the weekend warriors, mid-range paddles can offer great balance. If you play routinely, go ahead and get that high-end paddle. In my experience, if you find that you love the sport and play more than twice per month, you'll quickly want to upgrade to the high-end paddle. It does make a difference.

The Importance of Grip Size for Tiny Hands

If you've ever tried to eat soup with a ladle or write with a jumbo pencil, you know how important it is to have the right grip size. The same goes for pickleball paddles.

Having a paddle with a grip size that's too big or too small can lead to discomfort, poor racket control, and even injuries. For adults, grip sizes typically range from 4 to 4 1/2 inches. Kids, on the other hand, will need a smaller grip size, typically around 3 1/2 to 4 inches.

To find your ideal grip size, hold the paddle as you would when preparing to serve, with the base of your hand resting on the handle's widest part. There should be a small gap, about the width of a finger, between your fingers and palm. If the gap is bigger, the grip is too large. If your fingers are touching your palm, the grip is too small.

Remember, while grip size is important, it's also a matter of personal preference. So try out different sizes and see what feels comfortable and gives you the best control.

DID YOU KNOW?

A pickleball paddle's surface texture can influence the ball's spin and direction.

Other Features

In addition to varying materials, paddles also come in various designs catering to different playing styles and preferences. Here are some differentiating factors:

- Weight
- Lightweight (less than 7.3 ounces): Allows for quick wrist action and is easier on the arm.
- Middleweight (7.3 to 8.4 ounces): Offers a balance of power and control.
- Heavyweight (8.5 ounces or more): Provides more power but can be more taxing on the arm.
- Shape and Size: Traditional paddles have a wide body, but there are also elongated ("blade" style) paddles that are longer and narrower, which some players prefer for increased reach and power.

- Surface: Textured surfaces offer enhanced spin and control, while smooth surfaces provide a consistent and clean contact for precise ball placement.
- Edge Guard: A protective frame around the paddle's edge, it provides durability but can also increase the paddle's weight.
- Sweet Spot: The location on the paddle's face where the ball is struck most effectively. Paddle design can influence the size and location of the sweet spot. The traditional paddles with a wider body tend to have a larger, more forgiving sweet spot than the elongated paddles.
- Aesthetics: Now, you might think this is a frivolous point, but hear me out. Pickleball is not just a sport; it's a lifestyle. And just like any lifestyle, it comes with its own fashion statement. Choosing a paddle color that matches your outfit (or your mood or your favorite sports team) can add a dash of fun to your game. So go ahead and choose a paddle color that reflects your personality. Whether it's a classic black or white, a neon green or pink, or a fancy design, your paddle is an extension of you. Plus, it makes it easier to spot when you leave it laying around!

Consider taking a look at Pickleball Central's comprehensive "Paddle Guide"[1] for further assistance in selecting the right paddle for you.

Remember, the "best" paddle largely depends on individual preference, playing style, and budget. It's always a good idea to try out different paddles, if possible, before making a purchase.

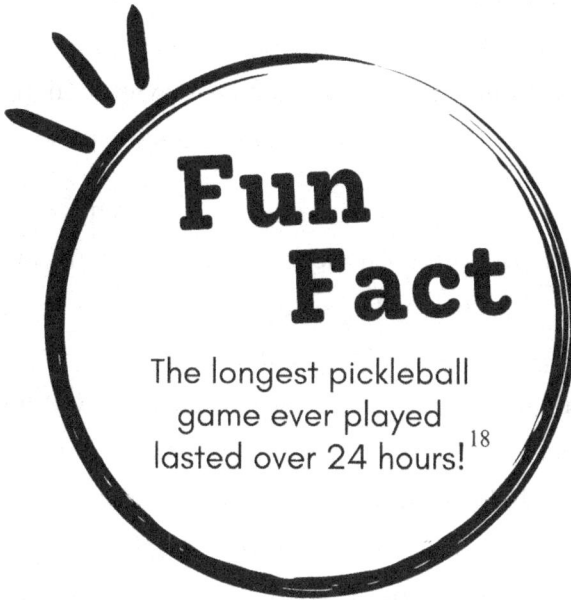

Fun Fact

The longest pickleball game ever played lasted over 24 hours![18]

OUTDOOR VS. INDOOR COURTS AND BALLS

In the world of pickleball, the playing surface generally dictates the ball type. Outdoor pickle ball courts are typically made of asphalt or concrete and then painted with a textured acrylic surface. This textured surface provides grip and helps reduce slipping when players are moving around, especially since outdoor environments can be exposed to elements like dew or light rain. The outdoor balls are designed to be tougher and more durable because of the rougher playing surface and exposure to external elements like UV rays. In addition, they have a thicker wall to withstand the rougher outdoor court surface and external environmental conditions. An outdoor pickleball typically has 40 small, precisely drilled holes. The pattern and size of these holes are designed to make the ball more aerodynamic and suitable for outdoor conditions where wind can be a factor. In addition, they are generally heavier, which helps the ball resist wind and maintain its course during play.

Indoor pickleball courts can be found in gyms or recreation centers and are often made of wooden gymnasium floors. Sometimes, they might be set up on multi-use sport surfaces like those used for volleyball, badminton, or basketball. These surfaces are smoother and softer compared to outdoor courts. These surfaces require a different ball type, called the indoor ball. Indoor balls have a slightly thinner wall than outdoor balls. Since they're used on smoother surfaces, they don't need to be as rugged as outdoor balls. They feature a smaller number of holes (often 26), which are larger in size than those on an outdoor ball. This design is for a calmer, more controlled indoor environment without wind. Additionally, the generally lighter ball allows for longer rallies and a slightly different style of play.

It's simple: pick your ball based on your playing surface, keeping in mind that not all indoor surfaces necessitate indoor balls. Depending on the playing surface, player preference, regional play standards, or specific tournament rules, outdoor balls can sometimes be used indoors but never the other way around.

WOW

There are professional pickleball players as young as 12 competing at high-stakes tournaments.

FOOTWEAR

Picture this. You're on the court, the game is heating up, and you're moving swiftly from one side to the other—when suddenly, you trip over your own feet and go tumbling down. Not exactly the kind of scoring you had in mind, right? That's where shoes come into play.

Now, pickleball is not a picky sport. It doesn't demand fancy gear or high-end equipment. But if there's one thing you shouldn't skimp on, it's a good pair of shoes. They're your trusty sidekicks, protecting your feet, providing support, and helping you move with agility and speed.

In short, your court shoes are your foundation. The grip, the cushioning, and the ankle support—they all play pivotal roles and are vital for preventing both immediate and long-term injuries. Shoes that fit snugly and reduce internal foot move-ment can cut down on excessive rubbing. Because pickleball involves quick side-to-side actions, it's advisable to opt for cross-training or court shoes over regular running shoes.

·Why did the ball get
expelled from
pickleball school?
For being a little
dill-inquent!

HA
HA
HA

If you're someone who's experienced persistent ankle discomfort or issues with balance, a laced ankle brace with added straps can offer the needed lateral support. Similarly, for those facing ongoing knee issues, a slim, supportive knee brace might be beneficial in ensuring comfort and steadiness.

THE IMPORTANCE OF SUNSCREEN AND HATS FOR OUTDOOR MATCHES

Let's move on to the unsung heroes of pickleball attire— sunscreen and hats. If you're playing outdoors, especially in sunny weather, these two items are a must.

We all love a bit of sunshine, but too much of it can lead to sunburn, dehydration, and more serious health risks. That's where sunscreen comes in. Look for a broad-spectrum sunscreen with an SPF of 30 or higher, and apply it generously before you head out to the court. And don't forget to reapply every two hours or more often if you're sweating heavily.

As for hats, they're not just a fashion statement. They provide shade, protect your eyes from glare, and help keep you cool. Look for a lightweight, breathable hat with a wide brim.

One last thing—don't forget your sunglasses. They'll protect your eyes from the sun's rays and help you keep your eye on the ball. Look for sports sunglasses that offer UV protection and have a secure, comfortable fit. And there you have it—your guide to the essentials of pickleball attire. Remember, it's not so much about looking the part but more about feeling the part. So, gear up, step onto the court, and let the games begin.

WOULD YOU RATHER?

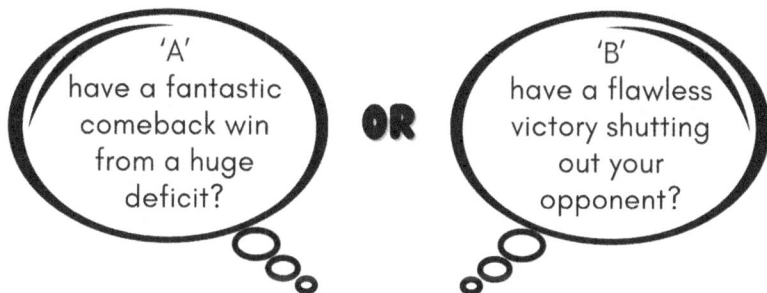

'A'
have a fantastic comeback win from a huge deficit?

OR

'B'
have a flawless victory shutting out your opponent?

PICKLEBALL EQUIPMENT CHECKLIST

Now that we've navigated the world of paddles and attire, let's take a moment to lay out the full spectrum of pickleball necessities. This handy checklist will ensure you're always prepared for a game, whether it's a spontaneous match in the backyard or a competitive tournament at the community center.

The Essentials: Paddle, Ball, and Enthusiasm

You can't play pickleball without a paddle and a ball—that's a given. But there's a third essential that's just as important, if not more so—your enthusiasm.

- Paddle.
- Balls (always carry a few extra balls in your bag).
- Enthusiasm: This one is easy to pack because it doesn't take up any physical space. But make no mistake, it's the most important item on this list. Your enthusiasm is what brings the game to life, what makes every shot a thrill and every point a celebration. So wear it like a badge of honor and let it shine on the court.

The Extras: Water Bottle, Towel, Snacks, and Sun Protection

Next up, we've got the extras—the items that might not be essential for the game itself but can make your pickleball experience a whole lot more enjoyable.

- Water Bottle: Pickleball is a workout, and staying hydrated is crucial. Bring a water bottle and refill it often. Staying hydrated will keep your energy levels up and help you play your best.
- Towel: Whether it's for wiping off sweat, drying your hands, or laying it down for a post-match picnic, a towel is a handy item to have in your pickleball bag.

- Snacks: All that running around is bound to make you hungry. Pack some healthy snacks like fruits or energy bars to refuel during breaks.
- Sun Protection: If outdoors, don't forget your sunglasses, sunscreen, and hat.

The Just-in-Case: First Aid Kit, Extra Socks, and a Good Joke

Last but not least, we have the just-in-case items. These are the things you hope you won't need, but you'll be glad to have them if you do.

- First Aid Kit: A basic first aid kit with band-aids, antiseptic wipes, and pain relievers can come in handy for those little bumps and scrapes that sometimes happen on the court.
- Extra Socks: There's nothing worse than sweaty, uncomfortable feet when you're trying to focus on the game. An extra pair of socks can be a game-changer.
- A Good Joke: You never know when you'll need to lighten the mood or break the ice. A good joke can be just the thing to bring a smile to your teammates' faces and keep the fun in the game.

Do you wonder what a professional pickleball player carries in their bag? Check out this video: What's in My Bag by Ben Johns.[2]

So, there you have it—your complete pickleball equipment checklist. With these items in your bag, you're ready to take on any pickleball challenge that comes your way. Just remember, while the gear can enhance your game, it's your skill, strategy, and spirit that really make the difference. So, gear up and get ready to play the game of your life!

Before we wrap, picture this: You're decked out in your new gear, paddle in hand, the net stands firm, and the ball seems to beckon. But wait, before you step onto that court, do you know how to serve, score, or even where to stand? Ah, but that, dear reader, is a riveting tale for the next chapter. [3]

ANNA LEIGH WATERS – IN 2019, SHE BECAME THE YOUNGEST PROFESSIONAL PICKLEBALL PLAYER IN HISTORY AT THE AGE OF 12. AS OF JULY 2023, SHE IS RANKED NO. 1 IN THE WORLD FOR DOUBLES, NO. 1 FOR MIXED DOUBLES, AND NO. 1 FOR SINGLES BY THE PROFESSIONAL PICKLEBALL ASSOCIATION.[10]

Anna Leigh Waters

CELEBRITY
spotlight

CHAPTER 3

THE PICKLEBALL BASICS – KNOW THE COURT AND GRASP THE GROUND RULES

P icture this: You're on a mission. A mission to conquer the thrilling world of pickleball. You've got your gear, you've mastered your paddle grip, and you're brimming with enthusiasm. But wait, there's one more thing you need—a roadmap to the rules of the game. Because, let's face it, even the most adventurous explorers need a map. And that's where this chapter comes in.

From scoring to serving, from bounces to bounds, we're going to break it all down—step by step, rule by rule. No jargon, no confusion, just plain and simple pickleball rules. So, buckle up and get ready for a fun-filled exploration of pickleball's ground rules. It's time to turn confusion into confidence, hesitation into action, and beginners into pros.

THE PICKLEBALL COURT

A pickleball court is a rectangular playing surface with dimensions similar to a badminton court, measuring 20 feet in width and 44 feet in length. The court is divided into two equal halves by a net that stands 36 inches tall at the sidelines and 34 inches at the center. The area closest to the net on both sides of the court is referred to as the "non-volley zone" or "kitchen," extending 7 feet back from the net. Players cannot hit the ball while standing in this zone unless the ball bounces there first. The court is marked with lines for the serving areas, which are further divided into two equal rectangles measuring 10 feet by 15 feet each. Service must be made diagonally, from one serving rectangle to the opposite serving rectangle on the opponent's side. The baseline sits at the end of each court half, and the sidelines run the length of the court, marking the outer boundaries.

The layout of a pickleball court is designed to facilitate fast-paced play, with the non-volley zone preventing players from smashing the ball right at the net, requiring a mix of strategy and skill.

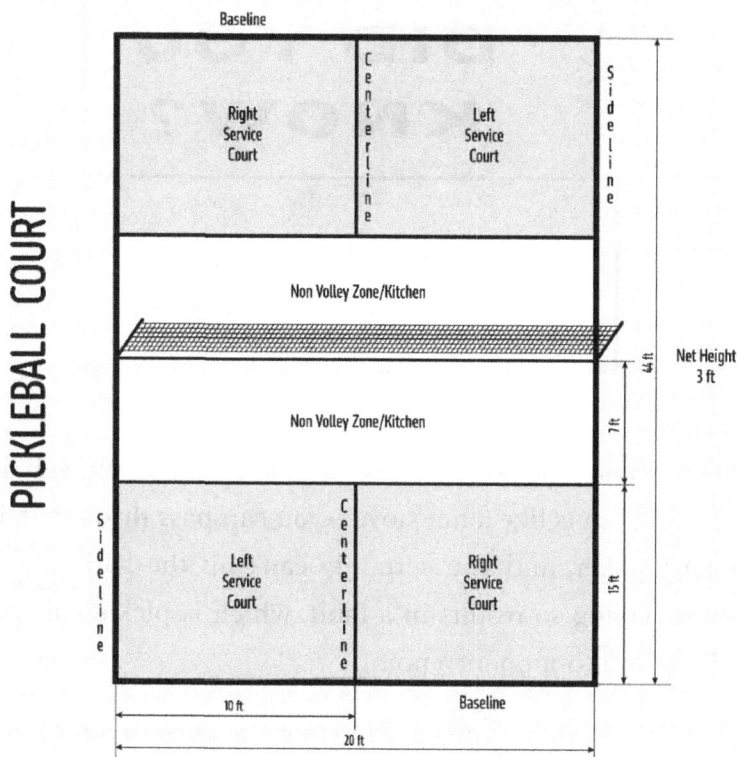

UNDERSTANDING THE PICKLEBALL COURT

The Importance of Staying out of the Kitchen

Now, if you're wondering why there's a kitchen on a pickleball court, don't worry; we haven't suddenly switched to a cooking show. In pickleball lingo, the 'kitchen' is a colloquial term for the non-volley zone, a 7-foot zone on both sides of the net.

DID YOU KNOW?

The "kitchen" is a term for the non-volley zone in pickleball.

So, why is it so important to stay out of the kitchen? Well, let's say the kitchen is like a hot stove—you can pass through it, but you can't linger, and you certainly can't hit the ball before it bounces. Doing so results in a fault, which is pickleball-speak for giving your opponent a point.

But here's the catch—you can step into the kitchen after hitting the ball, as long as it's not a volley. It's a bit like playing hopscotch with an imaginary line that you can and can't cross, depending on the situation. Sounds fun, doesn't it?

Knowing Your Boundaries

On a pickleball court, boundaries are your best friends. They're like invisible guides, helping you navigate the court and plan your strategy. Knowing where to place your shots and how to use the entire court to your advantage is a skill that comes with practice and an understanding of the boundaries.

The court is divided into several parts—the left and right service courts, the non-volley zone, or 'kitchen,' and the baseline and sideline boundaries. Each of these areas plays a crucial role in the game, and knowing how they work can up your pickleball game.

So, how can you make boundaries your secret weapon? By practicing shots that land close to the boundaries, forcing your opponents to scramble, and aiming your serves to the farthest corners of the service box. Remember, in pickleball, boundaries aren't limits; they're opportunities.

SCORING EXPLAINED

If the thought of scoring gives you flashbacks of complicated math problems or convoluted board games, take a deep breath and relax. Scoring in pickleball is as simple as counting to 11. Yes, you heard that right. No advanced math, no chess-like strategies, simply good old counting.

Here's how it works. You score a point when you win a rally while serving. Easy, right? The game continues until one side reaches 11 points and leads by at least 2 points. If both teams reach 10 points, the game becomes a nail-biting race to gain a 2-point lead. It's like a suspense thriller, where every point counts, and every serve could be a game-changer.

In pickleball, the flow of play is dictated by distinct serving rules. The game begins with the player on the right-hand side of the court, who serves diagonally to the opponent's side. The serve must be underhand, and the ball has to bounce once on each side before volleys (hitting the ball without letting it bounce) are allowed. Only the serving team can score points, and players alternate serves.

In doubles, each player gets to serve before the serve shifts to the opposing team. After the first serve of the game, both members of the team get a chance to serve, and play alternates between the two sides. The server continues to serve until a point is lost, at which time the serve passes to the teammate or the opposing team. This unique serve rotation ensures each player gets an equal opportunity to serve and play, maintaining a fast-paced and engaging game dynamic.

The scoring system is unique and is typically announced aloud before each serve to keep all players informed. The score consists of three numbers: the serving team's score, the receiving team's score, and the server number (either 1 or 2, depending on which player on the serving team is serving).

For example, a score announcement might sound like "4–3–1." In this case, the serving team has 4 points, the receiving team has 3 points, and the current server is the first server on their team.

Let's see how this might work in action. In this short hypothetical game, let's consider a doubles match where Team A consists of players A1 and A2, and Team B has players B1 and B2. The game starts with player A1 serving to player B1. Here's how the game might proceed with the score announcement:

1. A1 serves to B1: "0–0–1" (no points scored yet; A1 is the first server).

- A1 wins the rally.
- A1 serves again.

2. A1 serves to B1: "1–0–1" (Team A has one point).

- B1 wins the rally.
- The serve passes to A2 because A1 lost the point.

3. A2 serves to B2: "1–0–2" (Team A has one point, and it's the second server's turn).

- A2 wins the rally.
- A2 serves again.

4. A2 serves to B2: "2–0–2" (Team A now has two points).

- B2 wins the rally.
- There's a side out since both A1 and A2 have lost a service turn. The serve passes to Team B. On a side out, the serve always goes to the player on the right side of the court, who then becomes player 1 for that round.

5. B1 serves to A1: "0–2–1" (Team B has zero points, Team A has two points, and it's the first server's turn on Team B).

- B1 wins the rally.
- B1 serves again.

6. B1 serves to A1: "1–2–1" (Team B scores a point).

- A1 wins the rally.
- The serve passes to B2, as B1 lost the point.

7. B2 serves to A2: "1–2–2" (Team B has one point, Team A has two points, and it's now the second server's turn on Team B).

- B2 wins the rally.
- B2 serves again.

8. B2 serves to A2: "2–2–2" (The game is now tied).

- A2 wins the rally.
- There's a side out, and the serve returns to Team A, beginning with A1 again.

The rotation of the serve and announcement of the score continue in this pattern throughout the game. Each player on the serving team gets the opportunity to serve and score points until they make a fault, at which point the serve either passes to the teammate (if they haven't served yet in that rotation) or to the opposing team.

In singles pickleball, the server is the only one who can score, just like in doubles. The service switches sides after each fault. The server serves from the right side of the court when their score is even and from the left when their score is odd. The scoring continues in this manner, and the first player to reach 11 points with at least a 2-point lead wins the game.

Let's see how this might work in action. In this hypothetical, we have two players: Player A and Player B. The scoring is similar to doubles but without the rotation between teammates since each player is on their own. Here's a short game scenario:

1. Player A serves to Player B: "0–0" (the game starts, no points scored yet).

- Player A wins the rally.
- Player A serves again.

2. Player A serves to Player B: "1–0" (Player A has one point).

- Player B wins the rally.
- Player B gains the serve.

3. Player B serves to Player A: "0–1" (Player B has zero points, Player A has one).

- Player B wins the rally.
- Player B serves again.

4. Player B serves to Player A: "1–1" (the game is tied at one point each).

- Player A wins the rally.
- Player A gains the serve.

5. Player A serves to Player B: "1–1" (still tied).

- Player A wins the rally.
- Player A serves again.

6. Player A serves to Player B: "2–1" (Player A takes the lead).

- Player B wins the rally.
- Player B gains the serve.

7. Player B serves to Player A: "1–2" (Player B has one point, Player A has two).

- Player B wins the rally.
- Player B serves again.

8. Player B serves to Player A: "2–2" (the game is now tied again).

- Player A wins the rally.
- Player A gains the serve.

Still confused? Better Pickleball breaks this down in their video Pickleball Scoring Basics – Make it Easy with Me, You and Who?[1]

So, don't let the fear of scoring keep you off the court. Embrace it, enjoy it, and remember—it's just a game. The real score is the fun you have and the memories you make.

CORE RULES

Fun Fact

Pickleball is one of the few sports that originated in the United States but is now played worldwide.

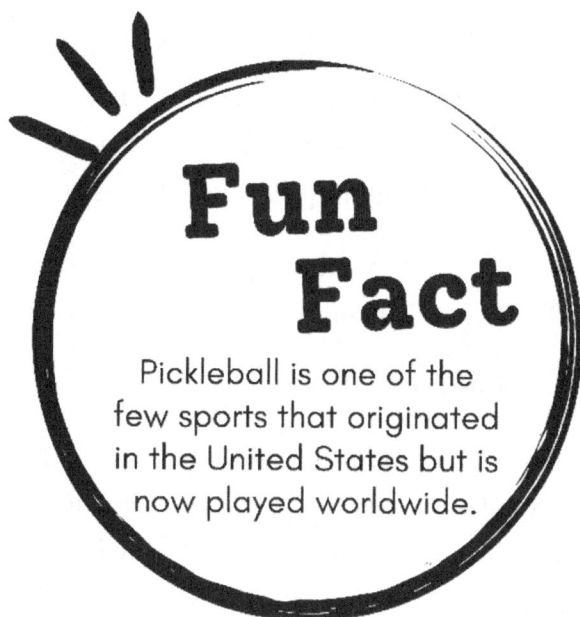

The Double Bounce Rule: Because Two Is Better than One

In the world of pickleball, there's a rule that's as quirky as the name of the game itself—the double bounce rule. Also known as the 'two-bounce rule,' it's one of the defining features of pickleball. And no, it's not a dance move, although it does add a certain rhythm to the game.

The rule is simple. Each side must let the ball bounce once before hitting it. That means, after the serve, the receiving team lets the ball bounce, returns the serve, and then the serving team lets it bounce again before playing their shot. After these two bounces, the ball can either be volleyed (hit before it bounces) or played off the bounce.

Think of it as a polite introduction at the start of each point, where the ball gets to meet the court before the rally truly begins. It's a rule that slows down the play, making it more beginner-friendly and adding a layer of strategy to the game.

Use this link for a video showing the Double Bounce Rule as explained by Better Pickleball.[2]

Stay out of the Kitchen

We discussed this earlier, but its importance cannot be over-stated, so it's worth examining again. The non-volley zone, affectionately known as the 'kitchen,' is a key player in the game of pickleball. It's a 7-foot zone extending from the net on either side and is the only area of the court where the ball must bounce once before being returned. Let's make sure this is clear. You can't volley the ball, i.e., hit it before it bounces, when you're standing in the kitchen.

This unique rule adds a dash of excitement to the game. It's a tantalizing area where you can reach the ball easily but can't volley it. It's a place that beckons you with opportunities but also presents challenges. In short, it's a place where strategies are made, points are scored, and games are won or lost.

The Non-Volley Rule is explained well in this video by the Pickleball Channel.[3]

SERVING RULES MADE SIMPLE

Serving in pickleball is like the opening line of your favorite song. It sets the tone, kicks off the action, and has its own unique rhythm. But unlike the high-octane serves in tennis or the spin-laden serves in table tennis, pickleball serves are underhand and, dare we say, a tad more elegant.

Why did the pickleball player fart during the serve? They were under a lot of pressure

HA HA HA

Here's how it works. Stand behind the baseline and hit the ball underhand, making sure your paddle face is below your wrist when it strikes the ball. The ball must be hit in an upward motion and served diagonally to the service box on the opposite side. One foot must remain behind the baseline until after the ball is struck. And remember, only one serve attempt is allowed, so make it count!

Check out this video on the Pickleball Channel for a visual of The Underhand Serve.[4]

The Intricacies of the Underhand Serve

Picture a child gently tossing a ball into the air and swatting it with a paddle. That's right, you've just imagined an underhand serve, the serving style unique to pickleball. This is not a game of wham-bam power serves. Instead, it's a gentle underhand swing that sets the ball and the game in motion.

But let's clear one thing up—just because it's an underhand serve doesn't mean it's child's play. Quite the opposite. Mastering the underhand serve takes skill and strategy. The serve must be hit from below the waist, and the paddle head must be below the wrist at the point of contact. The server has the option to drop the ball and hit after the bounce, or hit the ball in the air out of the hand; either is acceptable.

The key here is to aim for consistency rather than speed. A well-placed serve that lands deep in the opponent's court can be more effective than a fast serve that's easy to return. So, practice your underhand swing, find your serving rhythm, and remember—in pickleball, the underhand serve is king.

The Importance of Keeping Your Feet behind the Baseline

Now, let's talk about the baseline, that faithful line that marks the boundary of the court. Think of the baseline as the starting line in a race. When serving, one foot must be behind this line at the point of contact. The other foot can be anywhere—inside the court, in the air, or even doing a little jig—as long as it's not touching the line or the court.

This rule ensures that all serves start from the same position, keeping the game fair and square. Stepping on or over the line before making contact with the ball is a foot fault and results in a loss of serve. So, keep an eye on your feet, respect the baseline, and avoid those pesky foot faults.

Here's a pro tip: Practice your serve while standing a few inches behind the baseline. This gives you a little wiggle room and helps avoid foot faults. After all, in pickleball, every serve counts, and you don't want to lose one because of a wandering foot.

The Art of Aiming for the Opponent's Weak Spot

In the grand theater of pickleball, serving is your opening act. It's your chance to set the tone, to catch your opponent off guard, and to seize the upper hand. And one of the best ways to do this is by aiming for your opponent's weak spot.

Everyone has a weak spot. Some players struggle with low balls, others with balls hit to their backhand. Some get flustered with short serves, others with serves that land deep in the court. Your job as the server is to identify these weak spots and aim for them.

But remember, pickleball is a friendly game, and the goal is to have fun. So, while it's okay to target your opponent's weak spot, it's also important to maintain a friendly, respectful attitude. After all, today's opponent could be tomorrow's partner!

The Pickleball Guy shares beginner-level strategies in this video: How to Serve: A Beginner's Guide.[5]

So, there you have it—a guide to the simple yet nuanced rules of serving in pickleball. From the underhand serve to the baseline rule to the art of aiming, serving in pickleball is a skill that's as fun to learn as it is to execute. So, step up to the baseline, take a deep breath, and serve up some pickleball magic. [6]

The longest pickleball rally is 16,046 and was achieved by the Rossetti brothers in Connecticut on October 10, 2021.[16]

THE STRATEGY BEHIND USING THE NON-VOLLEY ZONE

So, what's the strategy behind using the kitchen? Well, it's all about control. By keeping your shots low and landing in the kitchen, you can force your opponents to hit upward, putting you in a better position to attack. It's also a great place to dink—a soft shot that just clears the net and lands in the opponent's kitchen, forcing them to hit a difficult return.

On the flip side, defending the kitchen is just as important. Quick reflexes, sharp anticipation, and a good understanding of angles can help you counter dinks and keep the ball in play.

Understanding and using the non-volley zone to your advantage can add a new dimension to your game, making it more strategic, challenging, and fun.

The Importance of Timing Your Steps

With its non-volley rule, the kitchen forces you to time your steps carefully. You can step into the kitchen after hitting the ball but must exit before the next shot if you plan to volley. It's a bit like dancing—you step in, hit the ball, step out, and prepare for the next move.

The key is to stay on your toes, ready to move in and out of the kitchen as needed. It's a test of agility, anticipation, and footwork.

The Pickleball Guy has a great introductory video: 7 Kitchen Strategies to Avoid Getting Crushed in Pickleball.[7]

WOULD YOU RATHER

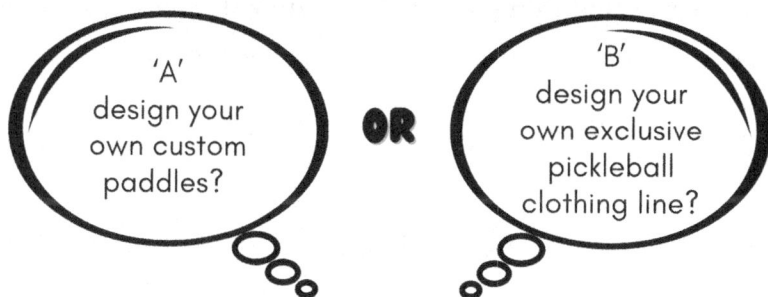

'A' design your own custom paddles?

OR

'B' design your own exclusive pickleball clothing line?

THE STRATEGY OF DINKING: IT'S NOT AS SILLY AS IT SOUNDS

If you're giggling at the word 'dinking,' you're not alone. But in pickleball, dinking is serious business. It's a soft shot that just clears the net and lands in the opponent's kitchen. The goal is to keep the ball low, forcing the opponent to hit upward and giving you the advantage.

Dinking is a game of patience and precision, often leading to a dink rally where players gently hit the ball back and forth, waiting for the other to make a mistake. It's like a suspenseful game of cat and mouse, where strategy trumps power and patience can win the game. It's not about the power but the placement.

The kitchen, with its dinks and unique rules, adds a layer of intrigue to pickleball. It's a place where games can turn around, where underdogs can triumph, and where each step, each shot, and each moment counts. So, step into the kitchen, embrace its challenges, and cook up your own recipe for pickleball success. And remember, the next time you're in the heat of a match, remember to cool things down with a dink. It might just be the secret sauce that spices up your pickleball game.

Check out 5 Steps to a Winning Dink by the Pickleball Channel.[8]

And there you have it—a sneak peek into the fascinating world of pickleball rules and strategies. So, stay tuned, keep practicing, and remember—the real joy of pickleball lies not in mastering the rules but in playing the game. After all, every serve, every shot, and every dink is a chance to make a memory.

So, step onto the court, embrace the game, and let the pickleball magic begin. [9]

KIM KARDASHIAN — RECENTLY TOOK UP PICKLEBALL WITH HER FAMILY AND HAS HELPED PROMOTE IT.[19] THERE ARE SEVERAL EPISODES OF KEEPING UP WITH THE KARDASHIANS IN WHICH KIM SHOWS OFF HER SKILLS WHILE PLAYING PICKLEBALL WITH FRIENDS AND FAMILY.

CELEBRITY spotlight

Kim Kardashian

CHAPTER 4

BEGINNER'S STRATEGIES FOR SUCCESS

A s a beginner, grasping the core elements of serve types, returns, third shots, and positioning can significantly uplift your game. This chapter is crafted to unveil the secrets of these essential tactics in a clear and concise way, tailored for novices. We'll explore a variety of serve options to initiate play effectively, unravel the art of crafting decisive returns, dissect the pivotal third shot strategies, and navigate through the nuances of optimal court positioning. Each section is infused with easy-to-understand instructions and practical tips to fast-track your learning curve. Get ready to elevate your pickleball prowess and step onto the court with confidence and skill!"

SMART SERVING STRATEGIES

Deep Serves

Picture a wide-open ocean. The deeper you go, the more mysterious and challenging it becomes. That's the idea behind the deep serve. You're aiming to send the ball as close to the baseline as possible. This puts your opponent on their back foot, giving you the upper hand. It's like challenging them to a game of catch; only the ball is always just out of their reach!

Short Serves

Now, imagine you're playing a game of tag with a toddler. You wouldn't run too far away, would you? You'd stay just out of reach, keeping the game fun and engaging. That's the short serve for you. It's a gentle drop just over the net, forcing the opponent to rush forward. It's the perfect serve to keep your opponents guessing and on their toes—sometimes literally!

Mixed Direction Serves

Imagine you're navigating a maze. You wouldn't just keep turning in the same direction, would you? You'd mix it up and keep it unpredictable. That's exactly what mixed direction serves do. Sometimes, you aim to the left, sometimes to the right, keeping your opponents guessing. It's a bit like performing a magic trick, where the fun lies in the surprise.

Power Serves

Ever tried to catch a fast-flying frisbee? It's not easy, is it? That's the power serve for you. It's a serve that packs a punch, making the ball zip across the court at a high speed. Just remember, power serves are like hot chili peppers—a little goes a long way. Use them sparingly, or you might end up missing the serving box more often than hitting it!

Slice Serves

Imagine slicing a loaf of bread. You wouldn't just hack it straight down, would you? You'd cut at an angle, creating a nice, even slice. That's the idea behind slice serves. By hitting the ball at an angle, you can make it spin, causing it to bounce unpredictably on the opponent's side. It's a serve that adds a little spin and a lot of fun to your game.

So, there you have it—a suite of serving strategies to add to your pickleball playbook. Each serve is a new opportunity to mix things up, to keep your opponents guessing, and to have fun. So, step up to the baseline, take a deep breath, and let the pickleball magic unfold. Because in pickleball, every serve is a chance to create a moment, a memory—a story worth sharing.

For a visual, check out these videos on different serve types and strategies: Deep Serves and Returns[1] and Slow Motion Serves with Top Pro Players[2] by PrimeTime Pickleball; Three Serves and Why You Need Them by the Pickleball Channel.[3]

MASTERING THE SERVICE RETURN IN PICKLEBALL

In pickleball, a unique aspect that sets it apart from many other racket sports is that the returning side often has an initial advantage over the serving side. This counterintuitive dynamic is rooted in the rules and structure of the game. Here's an exploration of this aspect.

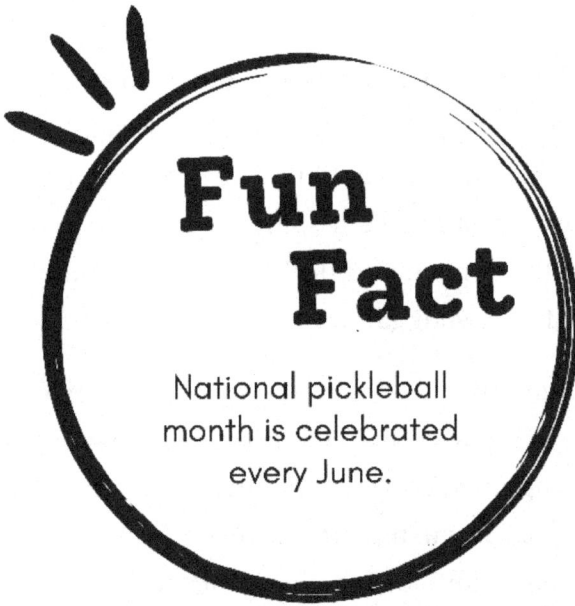

Fun Fact

National pickleball month is celebrated every June.

When the serving side initiates play, both players must remain behind the baseline until the ball is served and the return has been hit. The serving team is not allowed to volley the return of serve (hit it out of the air without letting it bounce), meaning they typically hit their next shot (the third shot) from near the baseline. On the other hand, the returning side can move forward immediately after returning the serve, allowing them to establish a position close to the net, which is the most advantageous spot on the pickleball court.

Holding the net position allows the returning side to easily volley the ball, making it difficult for the serving side to advance forward. The serving team often employs strategies like the third shot drop or third shot drive to neutralize this advantage and safely approach the net.

Essentially, the returning team starts with the positional advantage, closer to the net, and can immediately put pressure on the serving side. The serving side must skillfully employ tactics to overcome this initial disadvantage and turn the tables to win the point. This dynamic adds a layer of strategic depth to pickleball, making every serve and return crucial to the outcome of the rally and the game. In pickleball, the advantage is with the returning side, not the serving side. An effective service return in pickleball can set the tone for the entire point, offering both offensive and defensive opportunities. One foundational strategy is positioning. Ensure you're ready to move in any direction, with your knees slightly bent and weight on the balls of your feet. Anticipate the ball's direction and speed to optimize your response time.

When returning the serve, aim deep into the opponent's court. This tactical move forces the server to move back, giving you ample time to approach the net and establish control. Aiming for the corners can be particularly effective, as it requires the server to cover more ground.

Additionally, control and precision triumph over power in service return. A well-placed, controlled return can effectively neutralize the server's advantage. Focus on your paddle's angle and your body's movement to ensure the ball's optimal placement.

Lastly, mix up your returns to introduce unpredictability. Alter the pace, spin, and direction to keep the server guessing. This variance can destabilize the server's rhythm, providing an advantageous position for you as the returner.

Implementing these strategies enhances your service return effectiveness, laying a solid foundation for offensive control and defensive readiness in the fast-paced game of pickleball.

Keep them deep and have forward momentum, as demonstrated by Wayne Dollard in his video Pickleball Quick Tip: How to Hit a Better Return of Serve.[4]

THIRD SHOT STRATEGIES

DID YOU KNOW?

There's a "third shot drop" strategy in pickleball which involves a dink shot that drops into the non-volley zone.

Mastering the Third Shot Drop

The third shot drop is a pivotal strategy in pickleball that can bridge the gap between a service return and gaining control of the net, a key position for winning points. It involves delivering a soft, arcing shot that ideally lands close to the net in the opponents' non-volley zone, forcing them to hit upwards. This gives the serving team an opportunity to advance to the net and assume an offensive stance.

The essence of this strategy lies in its execution. The shot should be hit with enough height to pass over the net comfortably but with enough softness to drop into the non-volley zone. The opponents are then compelled to return the ball on the bounce, often lifting it high enough to provide the serving team with a potential winning shot.

Practicing the third-shot drop is crucial. Mastering the required touch and precision can transform this tactic into a powerful weapon in your pickleball arsenal. By successfully implementing the third shot drop, players can transition from defense to offense smoothly, making it a cornerstone strategy for both novice and experienced players aiming to elevate their game.

Each successful third-shot drop opens a window of opportunity to take control of the net, pressure the opponents, and, ultimately, win more points. By mastering this technique, players can significantly enhance their strategic gameplay, turning potentially defensive scenarios into offensive opportunities.

Unleashing the Third Shot Drive

The third shot drive in pickleball serves as an alternative to the well-known third shot drop. While the third shot drop is about finesse and placement, the third shot drive focuses on speed and power. This aggressive approach is used to apply immediate pressure on the opponents, giving them less time to react and forcing them into a defensive position.

Execution of the third shot drive involves striking the ball firmly and directly at the opponents, aiming to keep the ball low. The objective is to limit the opponents' options for a return, ideally resulting in a high, defensive shot that can be attacked with a volley. It can be particularly effective against opponents who are less adept at handling fast-paced shots or are positioned too close to the net.

However, the third shot drive isn't without its risks. A well-executed drive can force errors or weak returns, but if not executed properly, it can result in easy points for the opponents or set them up for a strong offensive shot. Thus, precision, timing, and decision-making are crucial to deploying this strategy effectively.

In essence, the third shot drive is an assertive strategy aimed at immediately seizing control of the rally. When executed with precision, it can be a potent weapon in a pickleball player's repertoire, disrupting the opponents' rhythm and creating opportunities to command the point.

The Pickleball Guy demonstrates these 3rd shot techniques visually and explains how to decide which to use in his video titled 3rd Shot Drop vs. Drive: Which to use and WHEN?[5]

POSITIONING FOR POWER

Court Awareness

Imagine being on a bustling city street with people hurrying in all directions. You wouldn't wander aimlessly, would you? You'd stay aware of your surroundings to navigate your way. Similarly, in the busy landscape of a pickleball game, court awareness is key.

Knowing where you are on the court, where your opponents are, and where the ball is headed can make a world of difference to your game. You'd want to place yourself in a position where you can cover the maximum area of the court. This gives you a better chance to reach the ball, no matter where it's hit.

Anticipating Opponent's Moves

Remember playing 'Guess the Move' with your friends, trying to predict their next step? That's exactly what you need to do in pickleball. Anticipating your opponents' moves gives you a head start, allowing you to be in the right position at the right time.

Look for cues—the direction they're facing, their grip on the paddle, and their body language. These can hint at where they might hit the ball. Remember, in pickleball, the game isn't just played on the court but also in the mind.

Strategic Positioning in Doubles

Playing doubles in pickleball is like performing a well-choreographed dance. You and your partner need to move in sync, covering the court without bumping into each other.

Typically, one player takes the lead, moving to the net, while the other covers the baseline. This allows you to cover both offensive and defensive plays. The key is to communicate with your partner, coordinating your moves to avoid leaving any part of the court exposed.

Optimal Position for Serving and Receiving

In pickleball, serving and receiving aren't just about the swing of the paddle but also about where you stand. When serving, position yourself such that you have the best angle to hit the serve deep into the opponent's court.

On the receiving end, stand in a ready position, balanced and centered, so you can quickly move in any direction. It's like being a sprinter on the starting block, ready to bolt at the first signal.

Quick Transitioning from Defense to Offense

Pickleball, much like life, can quickly switch from calm to chaotic and back. One moment, you're on the defense, backpedaling to return a powerful shot, and the next moment, you see an opportunity to attack.

Practice quick transitions from defense to offense. This could mean moving swiftly from the baseline to the net or switching your grip to hit a volley. It's these quick transitions that can catch your opponents off guard and turn the tide in your favor.

In the grand theater of pickleball, positioning is a powerful tool. It's your secret weapon, your game plan, and your route to victory. So, as you step onto the court, remember to stay aware, anticipate, strategize, position yourself optimally, and transition quickly. It's not just about how well you hit the ball but also about where you are when you hit it. So, move wisely, play smartly, and let your positioning power your pickleball play.

John Cincola explains the importance of court positioning and awareness in his video Court Positioning Fundamentals, You Can't Play Great Pickleball Unless You're in the Right Spot.[6]

There's an ongoing push to include pickleball in the Olympic Games. It could be an Olympic sport sooner than we think!

CONTROL OVER CHAOS: KEEPING COOL IN HEATED EXCHANGES

Breathing Techniques

Take a deep breath in. Let it out slowly. Feel better? Well, that's the power of your breath. It's your built-in stress reliever, your personal chill-out button. In the middle of a heated pickleball match, your breath can be your anchor, helping you stay calm and focused.

But how do you tap into this power? It's all about mindful breathing. Take slow, deep breaths in through your nose, hold for a moment, and then exhale slowly through your mouth. This kind of breathing helps slow down your heart rate, relax your muscles, and clear your mind.

Next time you're on the court and the tension is mounting, take a moment to focus on your breath. You'll be surprised at how much difference it can make.

Mental Visualization

Imagine you're on a tranquil beach, with waves gently lapping at your feet and a cool breeze ruffling your hair. Sounds relaxing, right? That's the power of mental visualization. It's your mind's mini vacation, a technique used by athletes around the world to boost performance and reduce stress.

In pickleball, mental visualization can help you prepare for a match, improve your skills, and keep your cool during intense exchanges. Before you serve, visualize the ball landing exactly where you want it to. Picture yourself playing a perfect shot, outsmarting your opponent.

Visualization not only helps you plan your moves but also boosts your confidence. Try it during your next game and see the difference it makes.

Positive Self-Talk

Ever noticed how we talk to ourselves during a game? "Oh, that was a terrible shot!" "I can never get this serve right!" Sounds familiar? That's negative self-talk, and it can be a real game spoiler.

Flip the script and try positive self-talk. Instead of berating yourself for a missed shot, say, "That's okay. I'll get the next one." Instead of doubting your serve, say, "I can do this. I've practiced this a hundred times."

Positive self-talk helps boost your morale, improves your focus, and enhances your enjoyment of the game. So, next time you're on the court, be your own cheerleader. You'll be amazed at the difference it makes.

Tactical Timeouts

In the heat of a pickleball match, it's easy to get caught up in the action. But sometimes, taking a break can be the best strategy. That's where tactical timeouts come in.

A timeout allows you to break the momentum, catch your breath, and regroup. It's a moment to hydrate, to strategize, and to reset. Use this time to reassess your game plan, discuss strategies with your partner, or simply to calm your nerves.

Remember, a timeout is not a sign of weakness. On the contrary, it's a smart move, a tactical advantage, and a power play. So, don't hesitate to call a timeout when you need it. After all, even the best players need a breather once in a while.

And there you have it—a guide to keeping your cool in the chaos of a pickleball match. From mindful breathing to mental visualization, positive self-talk to tactical timeouts, these techniques can help you navigate the highs and lows of the game with grace and confidence. So, step onto the court, trust in your skills, and remember—in pickleball, keeping your cool is half the game.

WINNING DOUBLES TACTICS

Effective Communication

Picture two dancers moving in perfect harmony, their movements guided by an invisible thread of communication. That's exactly what you and your partner need to emulate in a pickleball doubles match. Effective communication is the glue that holds a doubles team together.

Whether it's a quick nod, a hand signal, or a whispered plan, every bit of communication counts. Talk about who will take the shot if the ball lands in the middle. Warn your partner about incoming balls if they have their back to the play.

HA
HA
HA

Why did the pickle lose the tournament? It couldn't cut the mustard!

Congratulate them on a great shot or encourage them after a miss. Keep the lines of communication open and clear. After all, a team that talks together wins together.

Role Division: Server and Defender

Consider a superhero duo—while one charges ahead, the other covers their back. That's how you and your partner should operate in a doubles game. With every serve, decide who will be the server (the superhero charging ahead) and who will be the defender (the one covering their back).

The server's job is to set up the play with a strategic serve while the defender gets ready to respond to the return. This division of roles ensures a balanced offense and defense, keeping your team ready for whatever comes your way. Just remember to switch roles with each serve to keep your opponents guessing.

Coordinated Positioning

Think of a well-oiled machine, with each part moving in sync with the others. That's how your movements should be on the court. Coordinated positioning ensures you cover the court effectively, leaving no space for the opponents to exploit.

Work out a system with your partner. If one moves to the left, the other covers the right. If one charges the net, the other stays back. It's a dance of sorts where you move together, always aware of each other's position. It's this unspoken understanding that can give your team an edge in the game.

Shared Strategy Planning

Imagine you and your partner are plotting a thrilling mystery novel. You'll need to plan the plot, decide on the twists, and work out the climax. Similarly, in a pickleball doubles match, shared strategy planning is crucial.

Discuss your game plan before the match. Identify your strengths and weaknesses and those of your opponents. Plan your serves and returns. Decide when to play offensively and when to hold back. A well-planned strategy can be your roadmap to victory. Just remember, the plan is not set in stone.

Be flexible and ready to adapt as the game unfolds.

And there you have it—a playbook of winning tactics for pickleball doubles. From effective communication to role division, coordinated positioning to shared strategy planning, these tactics can transform your doubles game. So, team up, plan your moves, and get ready to rule the court. After all, pickleball is not just about the shots you play but also about the partner you play with. Before you move on, check out this video: 6 Pickleball Doubles Strategies New Players MUST Know by the Pickleball Guy.[7]

WOULD YOU RATHER

'A'
Would you rather be interviewed as a pickleball pro on ESPN?

OR

'B'
have your skills go viral on YouTube?

As we wrap up this chapter, remember that every serve, every shot, and every strategy is a step toward becoming a better player. So, embrace learning, enjoy the process, and, most importantly, have fun. After all, at the heart of every pickleball game is a simple goal—to enjoy the game and make some great memories. Now, as we turn the page to the next chapter, let's keep that goal in mind. After all, pickleball is not just a sport; it's a celebration of fun, friendship, and family. So, let's keep the celebration going—one serve, one shot, one game at a time. [8]

Ben Johns

CELEBRITY spotlight

BEN JOHNS – BEN TURNED PRO AT THE AGE OF 16 IN 2016, AND AS OF JULY 2023 IS RANKED NO. 1 IN THE WORLD FOR DOUBLES, NO. 1 FOR MIXED DOUBLES, AND NO. 1 FOR SINGLES BY THE PROFESSIONAL PICKLEBALL ASSOCIATION. HE FREQUENTLY PARTNERS WITH ANNA LEIGH WATERS FOR MIXED DOUBLES AND IS KNOWN FOR HIS POWER AND ATHLETICISM.[27]

SHARE THE FUN OF PICKLEBALL WITH FAMILIES ACROSS THE GLOBE!

"Sorry tennis, I'm with pickleball now." –

— *ANONYMOUS*

I hope that by now you've already headed to the pickleball courts for your first game! If you have, then you will undoubtedly have been surprised at how easy, fun, and dynamic it is.

There's good reason why pickleball has risen in popularity like bubbles in champagne. It's easy to learn, and you can hone your technique as you play. In the first few chapters of this book, you discovered a host of useful strategies – from how to deliver a killer power serve to how to position yourself for power. Pickleball is a game of precision, but this skill is easy to improve if you practice regularly.

My greatest hope is that pickleball has provided you and your family with a good reason to get outside and spend time together – free from the binds of screens and other technological devices. If this sport is already helping you build amazing new memories with your loved ones, I would love it if you could encourage other families to try it out too.

In under a minute, you can leave an Amazon review that will resonate with someone just like you.

Let others know that even someone who has never been into racquet or paddle sports can make immense strides in pickle-ball after just a few games.

Inspire them to head to a pickleball court with confidence by sharing your own story and your opinion on this book.

Thank you for spreading the word. My aim is for many more families to discover the joy of sport in the Great Outdoors amidst the people they love.

Scan the QR code below

CHAPTER 5

PRACTICE MAKES PERFECT – DRILLS TO ELEVATE YOUR PICKLEBALL GAME

L ife is like a jar of pickles; sometimes you're sweet, sometimes you're sour, and sometimes you find yourself in a bit of a pickle. But fear not! Just like you can fish out that stuck pickle with a bit of persistence and a good fork, you can also improve your pickleball skills with dedication and the right drills.

If the thought of drills takes you back to high school gym class, don't worry. These drills are nothing like doing infinite laps around a track or climbing a scary rope hanging from the ceiling. They're fun, practical, and designed to make you a better pickleball player—one shot at a time.

DRILLS TO ENHANCE ACCURACY

Target Practice

DID YOU KNOW?

The USAPA published the first rulebook for pickleball in March 1984.

Remember playing darts at the local fair, aiming for that bull's-eye to win the giant teddy bear? Well, target practice in pickleball is kind of like that—only, instead of darts, we use a pickleball, and instead of a dartboard, we have the pickleball court.

Here's how it works: set up targets at different areas of the court, such as near the baseline, in the service boxes, or close to the net. The targets can be anything—cones, hula hoops, water bottles, or even those old CDs you found while spring cleaning. Then, take turns serving or hitting the ball, aiming for the targets.

This is a great way to improve your shot accuracy and precision. Plus, it's a lot of fun, especially if you turn it into a competition. The one who hits the most targets gets to pick the next family movie night flick, perhaps?

Serve and Return Drill

Think of the last time you played ping pong, sending the ball back and forth in a rhythmic rally. The serve and return drill in pickleball is similar. It's all about getting the ball over the net, into the opponent's court, and keeping the rally going.

Pair up with a partner and stand on opposite sides of the net. One player serves, and the other returns the serve. The server then lets the ball bounce once before returning it. The goal is to continue the rally for as long as possible, focusing on accuracy and control rather than speed or power.

This drill helps improve your serve, return, and volley skills while also enhancing your control and ball placement. And who knows? You might just beat your personal rally record!

Cross-Court Drill

Picture a chessboard with its alternating black and white squares. Now, imagine playing a game where your bishop can only move diagonally across the black squares. That's similar to the cross-court drill in pickleball.

In this drill, two players stand diagonally across from each other, one at the right service court and the other at the left. They rally the ball back and forth, aiming to keep it within their diagonal half of the court.

The cross-court drill helps improve your shot accuracy, ball placement, and footwork. It also forces you to hit the ball at different angles, adding another layer of challenge to the game.

So, put on your thinking cap, grab your paddle, and get ready to conquer the pickleball court, one diagonal shot at a time.

DRILLS TO BOOST BALL CONTROL

Dinking Drill

Imagine you're playing a game of mini golf, with each hole presenting a new challenge. You have to navigate slopes, avoid obstacles and, sometimes, make the ball travel through a wind-mill! The key to winning? Control. That's the concept behind the dinking drill.

Fun Fact

The APP Tour hosted its first pro tournament with a $50,000 prize purse in 2018.

"Dinking," despite its funny name, is a critical skill in pickleball. Remember, it's a soft shot that just clears the net, forcing your opponent to scramble forward. The dinking drill helps you master this skill, allowing you to place the ball with precision and finesse.

To do this drill, pair up with a partner and stand at opposite ends of the net in the non-volley zone, or 'kitchen.' Gently volley the ball back and forth, keeping it within the kitchen. The challenge is to keep the rally going without letting the ball bounce or hit the net. It's a test of patience, control, and a soft touch.

Volley Drill

Think back to the last time you played catch with a frisky puppy. The ball barely touches the ground before it's caught and tossed back. That's the spirit of the volley drill in pickleball!

The volley is a shot that's hit before the ball bounces. It's a quick, reflexive move that can catch your opponent off guard and score some serious points. The volley drill helps you develop this skill, sharpening your reflexes and improving your hand-eye coordination.

Pair up with a partner and stand on opposite sides of the net. One player throws the ball to the other, who volleys it back without letting it bounce. Start slow, and gradually increase the speed as you get more comfortable. Remember, it's not about power but control and timing.

Wall Rebound Drill

Remember the hours of fun you had as a kid bouncing a ball off the wall? Well, who says you can't do that as an adult? The wall rebound drill brings back the joy of that simple game, with the added benefit of improving your pickleball skills.

What is the pickleball players favorite song?

HA HA HA

Hit me with your best shot!

All you need for this drill is a wall and a pickleball. Stand about 10 feet from the wall and hit the ball against it, letting it bounce once before hitting it again. Try to keep the rally going for as long as you can.

This drill helps improve your ball control, reaction time, and accuracy. It's also a great way to practice different shots, like the forehand, backhand, and volley. So, find a wall, grab your paddle, and get ready to relive those childhood memories, pickleball style.

There you have it—a trio of drills designed to boost your ball control. Remember, control is not just about the shots you play but also how you play them. It's about using finesse, not force; strategy, not speed; patience, not power. So, give these drills a try, and watch as your pickleball game rises to a whole new level of control and precision.

The 2022 Margaritaville USA Pickleball National Championships had over 2,300 registered players.

DRILLS FOR SPEED AND AGILITY

Ladder Drills

Just like a musician practices scales to fine-tune their skills, a pickleball player can use ladder drills to boost speed and agility. No, we won't be climbing any real ladders here. A speed ladder, lying flat on the ground, is all you need for this exercise.

Picture yourself standing at the start of the ladder, about to dash through it like a hamster in a maze. The goal? To step in and out of the ladder squares as quickly as possible. This could be a simple one-foot-in-each-square pattern, a lateral in-and-out shuffle, or even a hopscotch pattern if you're feeling particularly nostalgic.

As your feet flit through the squares, you're not just burning calories and getting a cardio workout; you're also enhancing your footwork, improving your balance, and boosting your agility. All these skills will come in handy on the pickleball court, helping you move quickly and respond to shots with lightning speed.

Cone Drills

Remember those thrilling car chases in action movies where the hero weaves through traffic, narrowly avoiding collisions? Well, cone drills are the pickleball equivalent of those high-speed chases, minus the danger and the dramatic background music, of course.

For this drill, all you need are some cones (or any objects that can serve as markers) and a bit of open space. Arrange the cones in a line, a zigzag pattern, or even a circle. Then, run, shuffle, or sidestep between the cones as quickly as you can.

As you zip through the cones, you're not just giving your heart a good workout. You're also improving your agility, coordination, and speed. These skills are vital in pickleball, where quick foot-work and sharp reflexes can give you an edge over your opponent.

Shadow Drills

Have you ever tried to outrun your shadow? It's quite the challenge, isn't it? Well, in pickleball, we embrace the challenge with a drill aptly named the shadow drill. But don't worry; you won't be chasing any actual shadows in this one.

Shadow drills are all about simulating the movements and shots you would make in a real pickleball game. Imagine you're on the court, facing an invisible opponent. Visualize the serve, the return, the volley, and the dink, and move as if you're actually playing these shots. You can even call out the shots as you make them.

This drill helps improve your speed, footwork, and shot technique. It also allows you to practice game scenarios and shot sequences, preparing you for real-life game situations. So, step into the imaginary court, face your shadow opponent, and get ready to play some shadow pickleball.

There you have it—ladder drills for footwork, cone drills for agility, and shadow drills for speed. Each one is a fun, effective way to boost your pickleball performance. So, gear up, set up your drills, and get ready to give your speed and agility a turbo boost. After all, in pickleball, every step, every swing, and every second counts. So, make each one count with these speed and agility drills. But remember, while drills can enhance your skills, it's the love for the game that truly makes you a winner. So, keep playing, keep improving, and, most importantly, keep enjoying the game. After all, pickleball is not just about the points you score but the fun you have, the friends you make, and the memories you create. Now, as we move on to the next set of drills, let's keep that spirit alive.

WOULD YOU RATHER

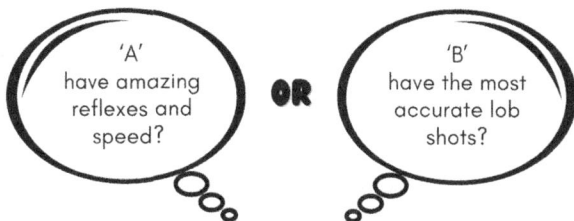

'A' have amazing reflexes and speed?

OR

'B' have the most accurate lob shots?

FAMILY FUN DRILLS

Round Robin Play

Have you ever been to a party where the music keeps changing and, with each beat, you find yourself grooving with a different partner? The 'Round Robin' drill in pickleball is a bit like that, only instead of dancing shoes, you wear your sports shoes, and instead of a dance floor, you have the pickleball court.

Here's how it works: Gather your family, friends, or whoever you can rope into a game. Everyone gets to play with each other, rotating partners after each match. It's a brilliant way to mix things up, learn from different players, and inject some friendly competition into the game.

The beauty of Round Robin play is in its spontaneity. You might find yourself playing with your grandma one match and your little cousin the next. It's a wonderful way to learn new strategies, adapt to different play styles, and, above all, bond with your family and friends. So, rally the troops, set up a schedule, and let the Round Robin games begin!

Skill-Based Games

Imagine you're at a carnival, trying your hand at different games. One moment, you're tossing rings, and the next, you're hitting targets. Skill-based games in pickleball have a similar vibe. They're designed to focus on specific skills while keeping the fun factor high.

Here's an idea: Set up a game where the only shots allowed are volleys. Or a game where every third shot has to be a dink. How about a game where you can only score points with a smash? The possibilities are endless, and so is the fun.

Skill-based games are a fantastic way to focus on improving specific aspects of your play in a relaxed, fun environment. They take the pressure off winning and put the spotlight on learning. So, pick a skill, create a game, and watch as your pickleball prowess grows with each playful match.

Mini Tournaments

Picture the grandeur of Wimbledon, the excitement of the Super Bowl, and the thrill of the Olympics. Now, bring that excitement home with a mini pickleball tournament. No, you won't have thousands of spectators or a shiny trophy (although a homemade one could be fun), but you'll have something even better—a day filled with laughter, friendly competition, and the joy of play.

Here's the plan: Set up a single or double elimination bracket and play short matches, maybe up to 7 or 11 points. Take breaks between matches for snacks, jokes, and some much-needed rest. At the end of the day, crown the winner and celebrate with a well-deserved treat. Maybe pizza, ice cream, or both!

Mini tournaments are a great way to experience the thrill of competition in a supportive, family-friendly environment. They're about challenging yourself, cheering for each other, and celebrating the spirit of the game. So, gather your family, set the date, and get ready for a pickleball tournament that's big on fun and high on excitement.

And there you have it—a trio of family fun drills that are guaranteed to amp up your pickleball game. Round Robin play to mix things up, skill-based games to level up your skills, and mini tournaments to bring out your competitive spirit.

Each drill is a celebration of play, an opportunity to learn, and a whole lot of fun. So, step onto the court, paddle in hand, and get ready to transform your pickleball practice into a family fun fest. Are you ready to play? [1]

Kevin Durant

CELEBRITY *spotlight*

NBA STAR KEVIN DURANT IS PART OWNER OF A MAJOR LEAGUE PICKLEBALL FRANCHISE AND SPENDS SIGNIFICANT FREE TIME PLAYING PICKLEBALL.[28] AT 7'5", SOCIAL MEDIA REFERS TO HIM AS THE TALLEST PICKLEBALL PLAYER. YOUTUBE IS LITTERED WITH VIDEOS AND SHORTS SHOWING KEVIN DURANT PLAYING THE SPORT.

CHAPTER 6

OVERCOMING OBSTACLES: TACKLING TRICKY SERVES AND MORE

In your pickleball journey, you'll face challenges that seem as formidable as a thundering serve from a seasoned pro. Don't fret! Just as a skilled returner reads the server's body language, adjusts their stance and grip, and crafts a return shot, you, too, can learn to tackle these tricky serves and other obstacles in your game.

TACKLING TRICKY SERVES

```
-☼-  DID YOU
       KNOW?

The APP has a "Next Gen Series"
of tournaments focused on 16–23
            year olds.
```

Reading Opponent's Body Language

Just like a dog's wagging tail or a cat's arched back can speak volumes about their mood, a server's body language can provide valuable clues about where and how they're likely to serve. Keen observation is your secret weapon here.

Is the server shifting their weight to one side? They might be preparing for a slice serve. Are they standing at an angle to the baseline? Chances are, they're planning a cross-court serve.

Learning to read these subtle signs can enhance your anticipation skills, giving you a crucial head start in preparing your return. It's like having a secret decoder ring that reveals the server's intentions.

Practicing Different Return Shots

In the diverse world of pickleball, there's no such thing as a one-size-fits-all return shot. A powerful serve might demand a defensive lob, while a high-arching serve could be ripe for an aggressive smash.

Picture yourself at a buffet, choosing the right dish to satisfy your hunger. In a similar vein, you need to build an arsenal of return shots and learn to choose the right one for each serve.

Spend time practicing different return shots—the drive, the lob, the drop, and the slice. Experiment with them during your practice matches. The more options you have, the better equipped you'll be to handle any serve that comes your way.

How do pickleball players say goodbye?

It's been a smashing time!

HA HA HA

Adjusting Stance and Grip

Imagine trying to catch a frisbee with stiff arms and flat feet. Not very effective, right? The same principle applies to returning serves in pickleball. Your stance and grip can make a huge difference in your ability to effectively return serves.

Adopt an athletic stance—knees slightly bent, feet shoulder-width apart, weight on the balls of your feet, and ready to move in any direction. Hold your paddle with a relaxed grip, ready to adjust based on the incoming serve.

Think of yourself as a coiled spring, ready to uncoil and respond to the serve with a swift, controlled movement. This readiness will not only help you reach the ball in time but also position yourself for an effective return shot.

Remember, the serve is just the opening salvo in the exciting duel that is a pickleball point. With keen observation, a range of return shots, and a dynamic stance and grip, you can transform the challenge of tricky serves into opportunities for winning returns. So, gear up, hone your skills, and get ready to turn those tricky serves into terrific returns!

Now, with the serve-return duel well in hand, let's move on to another common pickleball obstacle—the non-volley zone, otherwise known as the 'kitchen.' But don't worry; this kitchen won't involve any cooking disasters or dishwashing duties. Instead, it offers a spicy mix of challenges and opportunities to stir up your pickleball game.

Fun Fact

The ERNE is a fun shot where the player steps out of the kitchen to hit the ball around the net.

OVERCOMING THE FEAR OF THE NON-VOLLEY ZONE

Strategies for Effective Non-Volley Zone Play

Remember playing hide-and-seek as a kid? The thrill of finding the perfect hiding spot, the anticipation as the seeker gets closer, and the rush of finally being found. Playing in the non-volley zone brings back that thrill, anticipation, and rush.

While you might be tempted to avoid the kitchen, stepping into it can give you a strategic advantage. This is where you can use dinks to put pressure on your opponents. By hitting soft shots that just clear the net, you can force your opponents to hit upward, giving you an opportunity to attack.

But what if you're on the receiving end of a dink? The key to effective kitchen play is patience. It's about waiting for the right opportunity, keeping the ball in play, and staying ready for the attack. So, step into the kitchen, embrace its challenges, and you might just find that it's your favorite part of the pickleball court.

With practice, understanding, and strategy, you can turn the kitchen from an area of uncertainty into a zone of opportunity. So, keep these tips in mind, step onto the court, and let's get cooking!

DEALING WITH FAST-PACED GAMES

Improving Reaction Time

Think about the last time you swatted a pesky fly. It required quick reflexes, didn't it? In pickleball, especially in rapid games, your reaction time is just as important. To enhance this, let's turn to a good old buddy of ours—the wall.

Find a wall and mark a target point. Now, stand a few feet away and toss a pickleball at the target. The goal is to catch the ball on its return bounce as quickly as you can. Start with a slower throw and gradually increase the speed. It's like playing a game of high-speed catch, only with a wall instead of a friend.

This simple drill can significantly enhance your reaction time, helping you respond quicker in fast-paced games. So, the next time you find yourself facing a flurry of shots, you'll be ready, paddle poised, and reflexes razor-sharp. Watch out, pickleball world; there's a new quick-draw player in town! [1]

Many believe Pickleball can help manage Parkinson's symptoms as it combines hand and eye coordination that is considered excellent therapy for those suffering from this disease.[29]

DEVELOPING A STRATEGIC GAME PLAN

Ever played a game of chess? It's all about strategy, isn't it? Anticipating your opponent's move, planning your counter, and thinking several steps ahead. Fast-paced pickleball games require a similar strategic approach.

Before the game, spend some time observing your opponents. Identify their strengths and weaknesses. Do they struggle with backhand shots? Do they favor a particular serve? Use this information to develop a game plan. Perhaps you could target their backhand or use a different return to counter their favorite serve.

During the game, stay flexible and ready to adapt your plan. Maybe your opponents change their serving pattern, or they improve their backhand shots. Be ready to adjust your strategy accordingly.

A strategic game plan can give you a significant advantage in fast-paced games. It helps you stay one step ahead, turning the speed of the game from a challenge into an opportunity. So, put on your thinking cap, plan your moves, and brace yourself for a thrilling game of speed, skill, and strategy.

After all, pickleball isn't just about how fast you play but also how smart you play. So, gear up, step onto the court, and let's play some high-speed, high-skill, and high-fun pickleball!

WOULD YOU RATHER

'A' be known for your "pickleball trash talk?"

OR

'B' be known as the most polite player?

HANDLING COMPETITIVE PRESSURE

Mental Conditioning Techniques

Picture your brain as a muscle. Just like your biceps or glutes, your brain needs regular workouts to stay fit. In pickleball, mental conditioning is just as important as physical fitness. But how exactly do you exercise your brain?

One way is through meditation. It's a bit like taking your brain to a spa—a quiet, peaceful space where it can relax and rejuvenate. Regular meditation can help improve focus, reduce stress, and boost confidence. Just find a quiet spot, sit comfortably, and focus on your breath. It's that simple yet incredibly effective.

Another mental conditioning technique is visualization. It's like a movie where you're the director, the star, and the audience. Picture yourself on the court, playing perfect shots, scoring points, and celebrating victory. This mental rehearsal can enhance your self-belief, improve your performance, and prepare you for the real thing.

Pre-Match Preparation

Do you remember the exciting anticipation you felt as a kid on the night before a big school trip or a birthday party? The same feeling can hit you before a pickleball match, only with a dash of nerves thrown in. To keep the butterflies in your stomach from turning into a whirlwind, pre-match preparation is key.

A good night's sleep, a healthy meal, and a thorough warm-up are essentials. But preparation isn't just about physical readiness. It's also about gearing up mentally. Spend some time reviewing your game plan, visualizing your moves, and setting realistic goals for the match.

Remember, preparation is not just about doing your best in the match but also about enjoying the experience. After all, pickleball is as much about the joy of the game as it is about the thrill of competition.

In-Match Adaptation Strategies

Imagine you're on a road trip, and you hit an unexpected detour. You wouldn't just give up and turn back, would you?

You'd adapt your route and keep going. The same goes for a pickleball match.

Despite all your preparation and planning, you might find yourself facing unexpected challenges during a match. Maybe your serves aren't landing as planned, or your opponent's shots are harder to predict than you thought.

This is where your in-match adaptation strategies come into play. Be ready to adjust your game plan, change your shots, or even switch your playing style to suit the situation. Stay flexible, keep your cool, and remember that every challenge is an opportunity to learn and grow.

Post-Match Reflection and Learning

You know that satisfied feeling you get after finishing a good book? It's not just about reaching the end but also about reflecting on the story, the characters, and the message. A pickleball match is a bit like that.

After the final point is scored, take some time to reflect on the match. What worked well? What could you improve? What did you learn about your game, your opponent, and yourself?

Take note of these reflections and use them to shape your future practice sessions and matches. Remember, every match is a chapter in your pickleball story, filled with valuable lessons, exciting plot twists, and memorable moments.

Ben Johns, the #1 Men's player in the world, shares his thoughts on the mental game in his video: The Keys to Gaining Mental Strength On the Pickleball Court.[2]

In the thrilling game of pickleball, handling competitive pressure is all about mental conditioning, preparation, adaptation, and reflection. These skills will not only help you perform better under pressure but also enhance your enjoyment of the game. So, take a deep breath, step onto the court, and embrace the thrill of competitive pickleball.

As the sun sets on this chapter, let's continue our pickleball adventure, ready to face new challenges, explore new strategies, and make new memories. After all, the real victory in pickleball lies not in the points you score but in the fun you have, the friends you make, and the journey you experience.

So, gear up, paddle in hand, and let's keep the pickleball magic alive! [3]

Miranda Cabieses

CELEBRITY
spotlight

PERUVIAN MIRANDA CABIESES FOUNDED FUNDACIÓN CABIESES TO PROMOTE PICKLEBALL IN PERU. SHE SERVES AS A WORLD PICKLEBALL SPORTS AMBASSADOR BY THE INTERNATIONAL FEDERATION OF PICKLEBALL.[31] SHE HAS ALSO CONTRIBUTED TO CLINICS IN VARIOUS LATIN AMERICAN NATIONS, INCLUDING VENEZUELA, THE DOMINICAN REPUBLIC, COLOMBIA, AND ECUADOR.

CHAPTER 7

A GAME OF LIFE: THE LIFE LESSONS PICKLEBALL TEACHES US

I magine you're tuning a guitar, adjusting each string to hit the perfect note. Now, think of pickleball as that guitar and every player as a string. To create a harmonious game, every player needs to be 'in tune.' This chapter is about the beautiful symphony that is team play in pickleball, the resilience built from losses, the power of persistence, and the tranquility that this exciting game can bring into our lives.

TEAMWORK MAKES THE DREAM WORK

DID YOU KNOW?

A strong mental game in pickleball can enhance focus, boost confidence, and improve decision-making under pressure.

The Importance of Communication

Picture yourself in a bustling city square, surrounded by sights, sounds, and a multitude of languages. To effectively navigate this scene, communication is key. The same holds true on the pickleball court, especially during doubles play.

Communication in pickleball isn't just about talking. It's about non-verbal cues, like a nod or a hand signal. It's about knowing when to step back and when to charge ahead. It's about signaling to your partner where you're going to hit the ball or which ball you're going to take. It's about planning your tactics together, discussing your strengths, and supporting each other through the challenges.

Next time you step onto the court, remember that your paddle speaks just as loud as your words. Make every swing, every step, and every glance count. After all, a team that talks together wins together.

Trust and Reliability in Team Play

Think back to the last time you were part of a relay race. The trust you placed in your teammates was crucial, right? You relied on them to run their best and pass the baton smoothly. In pickleball doubles, trust and reliability are just as crucial.

When you're on the court, your partner is your ally. You need to trust them to cover their part of the court, to back you up when you miss a shot, and to work with you to outplay your opponents. Similarly, your partner needs to be able to rely on you to do the same.

Remember, consistency is key to building trust and reliability. So, show up, give your best, and be the kind of player you would want as a partner.

Shared Goals and Collective Effort

Ever tried to piece together a jigsaw puzzle? Each piece has a role to play, contributing to the bigger picture. In pickleball doubles, each player is like a piece of the puzzle, working together to reach a shared goal.

Whether it's scoring a certain number of points, mastering a new strategy, or simply having fun, having shared goals can enhance your teamwork and make your game more enjoyable. It gives you a common purpose, a collective mission, and a shared dream.

So, before you start your next game, take a moment to discuss your goals with your partner. Remember, it's the shared victories, the collective efforts, and the mutual dreams that make pickleball doubles a truly rewarding experience.

And there you have it—a peek into the beautiful dance that is teamwork in pickleball. From effective communication to trust and reliability, shared goals, and collective effort, team play in pickleball is a microcosm of the larger game of life. So, team up, tune up, and get ready to create a symphony of pickleball magic.

EMBRACING FAILURE AND LEARNING FROM LOSS

Viewing Loss as a Learning Opportunity

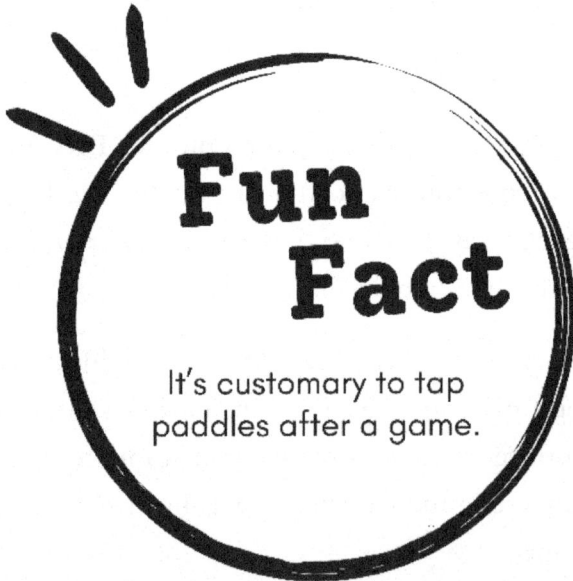

Fun Fact

It's customary to tap paddles after a game.

Imagine you're on a hike, and you take the wrong turn. You'd probably feel a bit frustrated, right? But what if that wrong turn led you to a beautiful hidden waterfall? Suddenly, that misstep doesn't seem so bad. In pickleball, just like in hiking, sometimes the wrong turn, the missed shot, or the lost game can lead you to unexpected discoveries.

Loss, as disappointing as it may be in the moment, can be a powerful teacher. It's like a mirror, reflecting back your strengths and weaknesses and offering insights that winning often overshadows. So, next time you lose a game, don't let the disappointment cloud the lesson. Look for the hidden waterfall, the silver lining, and the learning opportunity. It's there, waiting to be discovered.

Developing Resilience through Setbacks

Picture yourself learning to ride a bike. Remember how many times you fell? How many scraped knees and bruised elbows you've had? But did that stop you? No! You got back up, dusted yourself off, and tried again. That's resilience, and pickleball offers plenty of opportunities to develop it.

In every missed shot, every lost game, and every setback, there is a chance to build resilience. It's about picking yourself up after a fall, about trying again after a failure, and about turning setbacks into comebacks. It's about realizing that in the grand game of pickleball, as in life, setbacks are just setups for comebacks.

So, embrace your setbacks, learn from your losses, and let them fuel your resilience. Because in pickleball, as in life, it's not about how many times you fall but how many times you get back up.

The Role of Constructive Feedback

Imagine you're at a pottery class, crafting your first bowl. It's a bit wobbly and a bit uneven. The teacher comes over, points out what you could improve, and shows you how. That's constructive feedback, and in pickleball, it's a vital part of learning and improving.

Constructive feedback is like a roadmap guiding you toward improvement. It highlights what you're doing well and what you could do better. It's not about criticism or judgment but about growth and development.

Whether it comes from a coach, a teammate, or even an opponent, constructive feedback is a gift. It's an opportunity to learn, to improve, and to become a better player. So, welcome it, appreciate it, and most importantly, act on it. Because in pickleball, as in life, feedback is the breakfast of champions.

There you have it—a fresh perspective on failure and loss. Remember, in the passionate dance of pickleball, every stumble is a new step, every loss is a new lesson, and every setback is a new start. So, don't fear failure. Instead, embrace it, learn from it, and let it guide you on your path to pickleball proficiency. After all, in pickleball, as in life, it's all about how you play the game.

Why did the pickleball player become a baker?

HA HA HA

They were great at slicing!

THE POWER OF PERSISTENCE

Overcoming Challenges in Skill Development

In the kaleidoscope of pickleball, every twist and turn adds new patterns and challenges. As you plunge into the exhilarating world of dinks, volleys, and serves, you'll often find yourself grappling with new skills that seem as elusive as a rainbow's end.

Think back to when you learned to tie your shoelaces, ride a bike, or bake a perfect batch of cookies. It wasn't easy, was it? There were knots that wouldn't hold, wobbly wheels, and cookies that crumbled. But you didn't give up. You kept trying, kept learning, and kept improving. That's the same attitude you need to bring to your pickleball practice.

Each challenge you face in skill development is an invitation to grow—to stretch your abilities, sharpen your focus, and strengthen your resolve. So, embrace these challenges, not as obstacles but as stepping stones on your path to pickleball prowess.

The Reward of Continued Practice

In the world of music, there's a saying that goes, "How do you get to Carnegie Hall? Practice, practice, practice." The same holds true for pickleball. The secret to mastering this fun-filled sport lies in three words: practice, practice, practice.

Look at practice as your passport to pickleball success. Every hour you spend on the court, every serve you hit, and every shot you play brings you one step closer to your goal. It's like planting a garden—with every seed you sow, every weed you pull, and every flower you water, you're nurturing your dream of a beautiful blossom.

But remember, the reward of practice isn't just about winning games or scoring points. It's about the joy of seeing yourself improve, the satisfaction of hitting a perfect shot, and the thrill of learning a new skill. So, keep practicing, keep playing, and keep growing. The rewards will follow.

Persistence in the Face of Competition

Think of a marathon runner pushing through the miles, keeping their pace, and staying the course. That's the spirit of persistence you need to bring to your pickleball game.

In the face of competition, it's easy to feel overwhelmed, to question your abilities, and to lose sight of your goals. But this is where your persistence can shine. It's about staying committed to your game, no matter how tough the competition.

It's about sticking to your strategy, even when the odds seem stacked against you. It's about playing each point with determination, each game with grit, and each match with unwavering resolve.

There is a surge in real estate developments featuring pickleball courts as a central amenity.

In the electrifying arena of pickleball, persistence is your steadfast ally, your shining armor, and your beacon of hope. It's what keeps you going when the game gets tough, what drives you to reach for your best, and what inspires you to rise above the competition. So, strap on your persistence, step onto the court, and play the game with all the passion, courage, and determination you possess. Because in pickleball, as in life, persistence is the heartbeat of triumph.

PICKLEBALL, PATIENCE, AND PEACE

The Role of Patience in Skill Mastery

Visualize yourself trying to master the perfect pancake flip. You'd likely end up with a few flops before achieving that satisfying mid-air twirl. Much like perfecting your breakfast skills, developing pickleball prowess demands patience.

Patience is your silent coach, guiding you through the ups and downs of learning, encouraging you to keep trying, and celebrating each small improvement. It's the calming voice in your head that says, "It's okay; take your time. You're getting better with each swing."

Embrace patience in your practice. Allow yourself the time to understand the nuances of the serve, the tactics of the volley, and the art of the dink. Patience, in its quiet, steady way, builds the foundation of your skill mastery. So, as you step onto the pickleball court, let patience be your guide, your cheerleader, and your trusted companion.

Cultivating Calmness amid Game Pressure

Imagine being in the eye of a storm. All around you, the wind is howling, and the rain is pouring, but where you stand, it's calm and quiet. That's the kind of calmness you want to cultivate in the middle of a high-pressure pickleball match.

Calmness is your shield against stress, your oasis amidst the hustle of the game. It's about keeping a cool head, even when the score is tied and the next point could swing the game. It's about maintaining a relaxed focus, even when your opponent is unleashing a barrage of powerful shots.

Calmness isn't just about reducing stress; it's also about enhancing your performance. A calm player can make better decisions, execute more accurate shots, and enjoy the game more. So, take a deep breath, calm your mind, and step into the eye of the storm.

WOULD YOU RATHER

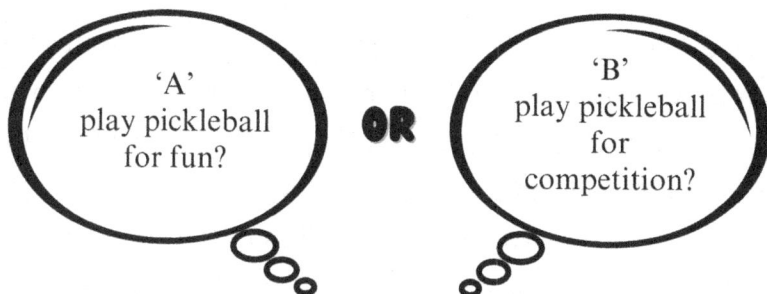

'A'
play pickleball
for fun?

OR

'B'
play pickleball
for
competition?

The Therapeutic Benefits of Pickleball

Picture yourself after a long, hectic day. Your mind is buzzing, your body is tired, and you're looking for a way to unwind. That's where pickleball comes in, with its therapeutic mix of exercise, fun, and social interaction.

Pickleball is like a natural stress reliever, releasing a cocktail of feel-good hormones that boost your mood, clear your mind, and relax your body. It's an endorphin-boosting, serotonin-releasing, dopamine-enhancing activity that's as good for your mind as it is for your body.

However, the therapeutic benefits of pickleball go beyond the biochemical. It's also about the joy of play, the thrill of competition, and the camaraderie of a shared activity. It's about the satisfaction of a well-placed shot, the laughter over a missed serve, and the shared cheer of a well-played game.

Pickleball, in its own playful, energetic way, is a form of therapy. It lifts your spirits, soothes your mind, and refreshes your body.

It's a reminder to embrace the joy of play, the beauty of sport, and the healing power of a good, hearty laugh.

So, as the sun sets and the pickleball court beckons, remember to pack a healthy dose of patience and calmness along with your paddle and ball. Because pickleball isn't just a game; it's a journey into the delightful realm of patience, peace, and playful persistence. It's an adventure that celebrates the joy of play, the lessons of loss, the power of persistence, and the harmony of teamwork. So, put on your game face, step onto the court, and let's indulge in the therapeutic magic of pickleball.

The court is set, the net is up, and a world of fun, fitness, and friendship awaits you. Let's play!

CELEBRITY *spotlight*

Susan G. Komen

IN 2022, SUSAN G. KOMEN® LAUNCHED PICKLEBALL FOR THE CURE TO "THE FIERCE AND FUN PICKLEBALL COMMUNITY WITH THE STRENGTH AND SUPPORT OF THE BREAST CANCER COMMUNITY." PICKLEBALL FOR THE CURE OFFERS PLAYERS OF ALL LEVELS, FROM BEGINNER TO ADVANCED, THE OPPORTUNITY TO PLAY PICKLEBALL WHILE RAISING FUNDS TO FIGHT BREAST CANCER.[32]

CHAPTER 8

THE PICKLEBALL COMMUNITY: YOUR NEW HOME AWAY FROM HOME

I magine you're at a grand family reunion. There's Uncle Bob cracking his age-old jokes, Little Timmy showing off his new bike tricks, and Grandma Betty sharing her secret apple pie recipe. There's laughter, cheer, and an overwhelming sense of belonging. Welcome to the pickleball community—your extended family, where everyone shares your love for this fantastic sport.

Whether you're looking to play competitively, seeking to learn from seasoned players, or just wanting to play for the sheer fun of it, the pickleball community is the place for you. It's where you'll find friends who become opponents on the court and opponents who become friends off it. It's where every game is a family gathering, every match is a celebration, and every player is a beloved family member. So, let's step into this vibrant community and explore the boundless opportunities it offers.

FINDING LOCAL PICKLEBALL LEAGUES

Identifying Suitable Leagues for Your Family

Just like your favorite ice cream parlor offers a myriad of flavors to satisfy your sweet cravings, the pickleball community offers a variety of leagues to suit your playing preferences. From beginner-friendly leagues to more competitive ones, from kids-only leagues to senior leagues, the options are as diverse as they are exciting.

Start by assessing your family's skill level and playing preferences. Are you beginners looking to learn the basics? An intermediate-level league with a focus on skill development would be a good fit. Are your family members competitive and looking to test their skills? Consider joining a competitive league that hosts regular tournaments.

Engaging with Local Pickleball Players

Picture yourself at a block party, mingling with neighbors, sharing stories, and forming connections. Engaging with local pickleball players is a lot like that. It's about reaching out, showing interest, and building relationships.

DID YOU KNOW?

Pickleheads.com has an extensive database of court locations in the U.S.

Attend local pickleball matches and events. Not only will you get to watch some exciting games, but you'll also get a chance to meet and interact with local players. Don't hesitate to ask questions or seek advice. Remember, every question is a stepping stone on your path to becoming a better player.

Benefits of Joining a League

Think of the last time you joined a club or a hobby group. Remember the sense of belonging, the shared excitement, and the collective learning? Joining a pickleball league offers similar benefits and more.

Being part of a league gives your family regular access to courts, structured play time, and a chance to participate in organized events. It provides opportunities to learn from more experienced players and practice your skills in a competitive yet supportive environment.

But the benefits of joining a league extend beyond the court. It's about being part of a community, forming friendships, and creating memories. It's about sharing high-fives after a well-played match, consoling each other after a tough loss, and celebrating personal milestones together. It's about the joy of belonging to a community that shares your passion, understands your struggles, and celebrates your victories—a community that feels like family.

CONNECTING WITH ONLINE PICKLEBALL COMMUNITIES

Navigating Online Pickleball Forums

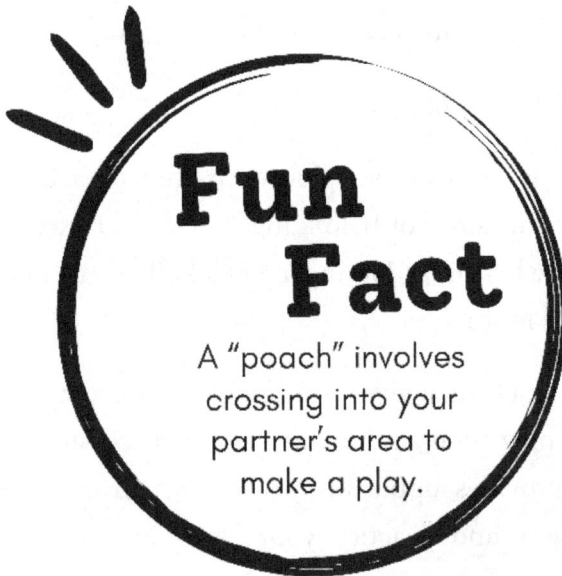

Fun Fact

A "poach" involves crossing into your partner's area to make a play.

Imagine stepping into a lively town square, where folks are engaged in animated discussions about their shared passion—pickleball. That's what online pickleball forums feel like—bustling virtual spaces where enthusiasts from across the globe connect, discuss, and learn.

These forums are treasure troves of information, advice, and experiences shared by players of all levels. You can find threads on topics as diverse as paddle selection, serve techniques, or even humorous pickleball anecdotes. It's like attending a global pickleball conference from the comfort of your home.

The key to making the most of these forums is active participation. Don't hesitate to ask questions, share your experiences, or even start new discussion threads. Remember, every interaction is an opportunity to learn and contribute to the global pickleball community.

Learning from Online Pickleball Tutorials

Recall the last time you learned a new recipe from a cooking video. The step-by-step instructions, the visual cues, and the ability to pause and replay—all made the process easier, didn't they? Online pickleball tutorials offer a similar experience, making skill acquisition more accessible and enjoyable.

These tutorials, often led by seasoned players or coaches, provide in-depth instruction on various aspects of the game. They break down complex techniques into manageable steps, demonstrate them visually, and often provide drills for practice.

Whether you're looking to perfect your serve, master the dink shot, or understand the rules of the game, there's likely a tutorial out there for you. All you need is an internet connection, a keen desire to learn, and maybe a notebook to jot down key points.

Participating in Virtual Pickleball Events

Think about the excitement of game night with friends, the friendly competition, the shared camaraderie, and the collective cheer for the winner. Now, imagine experiencing all of that, pickleball style, right from your living room. Welcome to virtual pickleball events!

These events bring the thrill of the game to your screens. From online tournaments and virtual coaching sessions to interactive webinars and Q&A sessions with experts, the variety is as impressive as it is engaging.

Participation in these events not only sharpens your skills but also keeps you connected with the pickleball community. It's like being part of a vibrant pickleball party where everyone is a click away and the celebrations never end.

So, whether you're a seasoned player, a curious beginner, or a family looking to add a dash of pickleball fun to your routine, the online pickleball community has something for everyone. It's a place to learn, to connect, to participate, and to contribute. It's your virtual pickleball family, waiting to welcome you with open arms. So, log in, join in, and let the online pickleball adventures begin.

PARTICIPATING IN PICKLEBALL EVENTS AND TOURNAMENTS

Preparing for Your First Tournament

Imagine you're about to embark on a thrilling roller-coaster ride. The anticipation is nerve-wracking but also exhilarating. Participating in your first pickleball tournament can stir up similar feelings. But don't worry; we've got you covered.

Start with setting realistic expectations. Your first tournament is less about winning and more about gaining experience. Focus on enjoying the game, learning from others, and absorbing the tournament atmosphere.

Next, ensure you're physically prepared. Regular practice sessions in the weeks leading to the tournament are crucial. They help you fine-tune your skills, build up your stamina, and get in the groove for competitive play.

Don't forget the importance of rest. Get a good night's sleep before the tournament day. This will keep you fresh, alert, and ready for action.

Lastly, pack your pickleball bag with essential gear—paddles, balls, a towel, a water bottle, and a change of clothes. And yes, don't forget to pack a healthy dose of enthusiasm and sportsmanship!

Understanding Tournament Etiquette

Stepping into a pickleball tournament is like entering a grand hall with its own rules of conduct. It's essential to understand and follow tournament etiquette.

Punctuality is paramount. Arriving well before your match not only allows you time to warm up but also shows respect for the organizers and your opponents.

Remember, good sportsmanship is the heart of pickleball. Acknowledge good shots by your opponents. Stay positive and composed, even if the game isn't going in your favor.

Avoid distracting your opponents. Once a rally starts, keep quiet, whether you're playing or spectating. Also, if a stray ball rolls onto a court, wait for the ongoing rally to finish before retrieving it.

Lastly, don't forget to thank your opponent and the referee at the end of the match. It's more than just a polite gesture; it's a reflection of your respect for the game and its players.

Post-Tournament Reflection and Improvement

After the adrenaline rush of the tournament subsides, it's time for reflection. It's like sitting down after a long hike, soaking in the experience, and pondering over the journey.

Start by assessing your performance. What worked well? What could be improved? Jot down these observations while they're fresh in your mind.

Next, seek feedback. If a coach accompanied you, discuss your matches with them. Their insights can be valuable in identifying areas for improvement.

Also, remember to reflect on the mental aspect of your game. How well did you handle the pressure? Were you able to stay focused throughout the tournament? Mental toughness is a critical part of pickleball, especially in competitive play.

Finally, use your reflections to set goals for your next tournament. Maybe you want to improve your serve accuracy, or perhaps you aim to handle match pressure better. Whatever your goals, ensure they're realistic and achievable.

Remember, every tournament, whether you win or lose, is a stepping stone on your path to becoming a better pickleball player. It's about learning, growing, and consistently striving to improve. So, take in the experience, learn from it, and let it guide you on your pickleball adventure.

Playing pickleball can burn more calories than walking, swimming, or bowling in the same time period!

GIVING BACK: VOLUNTEERING IN THE PICKLEBALL WORLD

Opportunities for Volunteering

Imagine you're at a county fair, bustling with people, laughter, and excitement. There's a popcorn stand, a Ferris wheel, a face painting booth, and, amid all that, a pickleball demonstration booth. That booth could be your chance to give back to the sport you love. Yes, the pickleball world is filled with volunteer opportunities just waiting for you to seize them.

From organizing a pickleball event in your local community to setting up a skills clinic for beginners to even offering to coach in schools or community centers, there are myriad ways to volunteer. Perhaps you could help maintain local pickleball courts or assist in a charity tournament. You might even consider starting a pickleball blog or a YouTube channel to share your knowledge and experiences with others.

WOULD YOU RATHER

 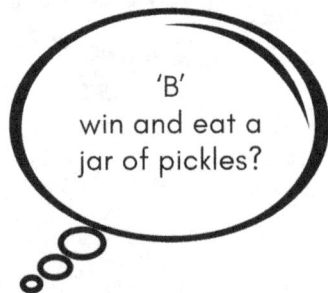

The Impact of Volunteering on the Community

Think back to the last time someone helped you when you were new to something. That little act of kindness probably made a big difference, didn't it? That's the kind of impact you can have when you volunteer in the pickleball community.

Your volunteering efforts can help grow the sport, making it accessible to more people. It can inspire others to take up the sport, improve their skills, or even start volunteering themselves. It can foster a sense of community, camaraderie, and shared passion.

But the impact of volunteering isn't just outward; it's also inward. Volunteering can be incredibly rewarding. It can enrich your experience of the sport, help you make new friends, and give you the satisfaction of contributing to a sport that brings joy to so many people.

Encouraging Family Involvement in Volunteering

Remember those fun-filled family camping trips where everyone had a role to play? Dad set up the tent, Mom prepared the food, and you and your siblings gathered firewood. Volunteering in the pickleball community can be a similar collective family adventure.

Encourage your family to get involved in volunteering activities. It could be as simple as helping set up for a local tournament, organizing a pickleball fundraiser, or even assisting in a community pickleball clinic. It's a great way to spend quality family time, bond over a shared love for the sport, and instill in younger family members the value of giving back to the community.

Just imagine the fun of running a pickleball booth at a local fair, the satisfaction of seeing new players enjoy the game at a clinic you helped organize, or the pride of watching a tournament unfold smoothly—thanks to your family's collective effort.

So, why wait? Step up, give back, and make your mark in the pickleball community. In pickleball, as in life, the joy of playing the game is amplified when you share it with others, contribute to its growth, and experience the satisfaction of giving back. When you volunteer, you're not just serving the ball; you're serving the community, and that's a game worth playing.

Now, as we flip the page to the next chapter, let's continue our exploration of the beautiful game of pickleball and the life lessons it teaches us. After all, pickleball is not just a sport; it's a way of life, a celebration of community, camaraderie, and shared passion. So, are you ready to continue this exciting adventure? Game on! [1]

CELEBRITY
spotlight

WE STUMBLED UPON I-MAN ON INSTAGRAM, AND WE JUST LOVE HIM. THOUGH NOT A SUPERSTAR YET, THERE'S AN UNDENIABLE SPARK IN HIM THAT MAKES US BELIEVE HE'S DESTINED FOR GREATNESS IN THE NEAR FUTURE. KEEP AN EYE ON I-MAN; WE'RE CERTAIN HE'S A RISING STAR IN THE MAKING! FIND HIM @CHRONICLES_OF_IMAN.[33]

CHAPTER 9

THE GENTLE(WO)MAN'S GAME – ETIQUETTE AND FAIR PLAY IN PICKLEBALL

Imagine you're at a well-coordinated symphony, with the musicians in perfect harmony and the conductor leading with an air of respect and grace. Now, transfer that scene onto the pickleball court. Each player, much like the musicians, has a part to play, contributing their skills, respect, and positivity to the melody of the game. Welcome to Chapter 9, where we'll uncover the unwritten rules of pickleball, the importance of good sportsmanship, and the art of managing conflicts on the court. The aim is not just to help you become a player who's admired for their skills but also one who's respected for their conduct.

On the pickleball court, as in life, how you play the game matters just as much as the outcome. It's not merely about winning points but how you win them. It's about playing with respect, integrity, and a dash of good humor. So, let's take a closer look at the invisible rulebook of pickleball and how you can embrace these principles in your game.

THE UNWRITTEN RULES OF PICKLEBALL

It's customary to tap paddles after a game.

DID YOU KNOW?

Don't Call the Ball Out Before It Lands is a key unwritten rule of pickleball.

Respect for Opponents and Officials

Think of a time when you experienced genuine respect—perhaps at work, from a colleague who valued your ideas, or at home, from a family member who appreciated your efforts. It felt good, didn't it? That's the power of respect, and it's just as impactful on the pickleball court.

Respect for opponents is one of the unwritten rules of pickleball. It's about acknowledging their skills, appreciating their good shots, and treating them with courtesy, regardless of the competition. It's about shaking hands at the end of a match and saying a sincere "Good game," whether you won or lost.

Similarly, showing respect to officials is crucial. They work hard to ensure fair play and a smooth game flow. So, whether you agree with their calls or not, it's important to respect their decisions and communicate any disagreements in a polite and constructive manner. Remember, without opponents to challenge you and officials to oversee the game, there would be no match to enjoy.

Maintaining a Positive Attitude

Imagine you're watching a comedy show. The comedian on stage is not just telling jokes; they're spreading positivity, making people laugh, and brightening their day. On the pickleball court, maintaining a positive attitude can have a similar effect. It can uplift your spirits, boost your performance, and even influence the mood of the game.

A positive attitude is about focusing on the enjoyable aspects of the game rather than obsessing over every missed shot or lost point. It's about smiling even when the game isn't going your way, laughing at your own mistakes, and appreciating the opportunity to play and learn.

Maintaining a positive attitude doesn't mean suppressing your competitive spirit. It simply means choosing a mindset that enhances your enjoyment of the game and showcases the fun, friendly spirit of pickleball.

Observing Court Boundaries and Rules

Picture yourself in a library. There are certain unspoken rules, aren't there? You speak softly, respect others' space, and handle books with care. Similarly, when you're on a pickleball court, it's important to observe certain norms regarding court boundaries and rules.

This involves simple things like avoiding encroachment onto an adjacent court during your match or retrieving a stray ball only when their game is paused. It also means respecting facility rules, such as using proper court shoes, keeping the court clean, and adhering to the scheduled time slots

Observing court boundaries and rules is about being a responsible member of the pickleball community. It's about ensuring a pleasant playing environment for everyone. After all, the pickleball court is not just a place to play; it's a space to foster camaraderie, mutual respect, and love for the game.

Call Out the Score before You Serve

It is customary for the serving player to announce the score before each serve. This practice is a sign of respect, as it helps ensure that all players are aware of the current score and signals the server's readiness. Furthermore, it helps prevent score discrepancies and confusion among players who may have different scores in mind before proceeding to the next point.

Don't Serve until Other Players Are Ready

It's considered a matter of common courtesy to wait until the other players are prepared before serving the ball.

Don't Call the Ball Out Before It Lands

Occasionally, you might feel tempted to declare a ball "out" before it touches the ground. It's best to avoid doing this. Such premature calls can be considered impolite, and it's important to remember that some balls may have a spin that makes their trajectory unpredictable. You cannot be completely certain that a ball is out until it actually lands and bounces.

Returning the Ball

If a pickleball ball becomes trapped on your side of the net and needs to be returned to your opponent, throw it back solidly to the next server. Avoid making them run, jump, or bend over to retrieve it. Additionally, it's a wise habit to keep a few spare balls in your pocket at all times. This will prevent you and your fellow players from constantly searching for balls during the game. Finally, always express gratitude to anyone who makes the effort to retrieve the ball for you.

ENCOURAGING GOOD SPORTSMANSHIP

The Importance of Fair Play

Imagine taking part in a friendly neighborhood cook-off. Wouldn't the victory taste much sweeter if you'd won based on the merit of your secret barbecue sauce rather than resorting to sneaky tactics like switching salt for sugar in your rival's kitchen? In pickleball, this principle applies as well. Playing fair is not just about adhering to the rules; it's about honoring the spirit of the game.

Fair play means respecting the serve, waiting for the ball to bounce twice at the beginning of each point, keeping your volleys out of the non-volley zone, and being honest with line calls. It's about understanding the game, enhancing the sportsmanship of players, and fostering a culture of respect and honesty in the pickleball community. So, the next time you step on the court, remember that playing fair is the first step toward becoming not just a better player but also a champion in the true sense.

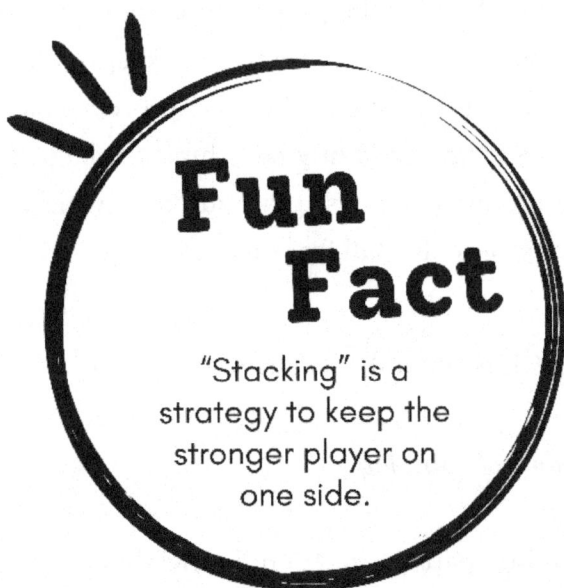

Fun Fact

"Stacking" is a strategy to keep the stronger player on one side.

Celebrating Opponents' Successes

Think of the last time you cheered for your favorite sports team, even when they scored a point against your home team. It was about appreciating a good play, regardless of who made it. On the pickleball court, celebrating your opponents' successes is a similar sportsmanlike gesture.

Did your opponent make a fantastic serve or pull off a skillful dink shot? Take a moment to acknowledge it. A simple "Good shot!" can go a long way in promoting friendly competition and mutual respect. It demonstrates that you appreciate skill and effort, no matter who it comes from. This kind of sportsmanship enriches the game, fosters mutual respect, and makes the entire experience more enjoyable for everyone. After all, pickleball is not just about winning; it's about playing well and appreciating when others do the same.

Handling Disputes with Grace

Imagine you're at a lively family dinner, and a heated debate breaks out about who makes the best lasagna. Would you flip the table in protest or engage in a calm discussion, respecting everyone's opinions? In pickleball, disputes are much like that dinner debate, and handling them with grace is key.

Whether it's a disagreement about a line call, a score dispute, or a misunderstanding about a rule, disputes are part and parcel of any sport. The key lies in addressing them calmly, respectfully, and objectively. State your perspective clearly, listen to your opponent's viewpoint, and seek a fair resolution. If you can't agree, consider replaying the point or seeking an official's opinion.

Remember, how you handle disputes can significantly impact your relationships with other players and your enjoyment of the game. So, next time you find yourself in a pickleball pickle, choose grace over grudges, dialogue over discord, and sportsmanship over squabbles. Because, at the end of the day, it's just a game, and games are meant to be enjoyed.

Avoid Giving Unsolicited Advice

It's important to avoid offering unsolicited lessons during a game, as it can come across as impolite. Giving advice without being asked can be frustrating and annoying for other players, especially if their primary goal is to have fun. To ensure a positive and respectful environment, make sure to ask players if they are interested in receiving any recommendations before providing them.

Don't Lob behind Players with Physical Limitations

In a competitive tournament environment, it's crucial to employ every strategy for victory. Yet, in casual recreational play, it's generally considered poor sportsmanship to lob the ball behind players with limited mobility and subject your opponents to injury.

Play at Your Skill Level

Be transparent and compete at a skill level that corresponds to your proficiency (e.g., beginner, intermediate, or advanced—as outlined in Chapter 10), whether you're participating in open community games or tournaments. Play at a different skill level only if you've received a specific invitation to do so, either to play at a higher or lower level.

Meet at the Net after a Game

In pickleball, it's customary to end a match by coming to the net. Players usually extend their paddles for a friendly "high five." To protect their paddle face or edge guard, some opt to offer the handle of their paddle instead of their face.

How does a pickleball player answer the phone?

"Yellow!"

HA HA HA

RESOLVING CONFLICTS ON THE COURT

Effective Communication during Conflicts

Picture yourself in a bustling marketplace, vendors and customers haggling over prices, the air thick with differing opinions. Amid this chaos, the ones who communicate effectively secure the best deals. On the pickleball court, conflicts can sometimes feel like that marketplace, and effective communication is your key to resolution.

Communication during conflicts isn't about raising voices but about raising points. It's about expressing your viewpoint clearly, listening to the other side, and seeking a mutual understanding. It's about using "I" statements, like "I saw the ball as out," instead of accusatory "You" statements, like "You made a wrong call."

Remember, conflicts are not battles to be won but problems to be solved. So, keep your communication respectful, open, and focused on the issue at hand. After all, the goal is not to prove who's right but to ensure that the joy of the game is not overshadowed by disagreements.

Seeking Mediation When Necessary

Imagine you're at a crossroads, unsure which way to go. A friendly local offers to guide you, pointing you in the right direction. In pickleball conflicts, seeking mediation can be like asking for directions at a crossroads.

When conflicts escalate or a resolution seems elusive, don't hesitate to seek mediation. This could be a referee, a tournament official, or even a neutral third party. A mediator can provide a fresh perspective, help clarify misunderstandings, and guide the parties toward a fair resolution.

Remember, seeking mediation is not an admission of defeat but an affirmation of fairness. It's about ensuring that the rules are upheld, the play is fair, and the game continues in the spirit of sportsmanship.

WOW

Pickleball courts multiplied from a few to over 10,000 in the U.S. in less than a decade.

Learning from Conflict Resolution

Think back to your school days when you learned something new. The first few times, it was challenging, but as you practiced, it became easier, almost second nature. Learning from conflict resolution in pickleball can be a similar process.

Every conflict presents a learning opportunity. It can teach you about the rules of the game, about your communication style, and even about your reactions under pressure. It's like a real-time, on-court class in problem-solving, communication, and sportsmanship.

Reflect on each conflict, not as a disagreeable incident but as a learning experience. What could you have done differently? How could you have communicated better? How can you prevent such conflicts in the future? Use these reflections to grow as a player and as a sportsman, turning every conflict into a stepping stone toward better understanding and improved play.

Conflict on the pickleball court, as in life, is not about the disagreement itself but how you handle it. It's about communicating effectively, seeking mediation when necessary, and learning from each experience. It's about turning the sour pickles of conflict into the sweet relish of resolution. So, the next time you find yourself in a pickleball conflict, remember it's not just a problem but an opportunity—an opportunity to learn, to grow, and to exemplify the true spirit of pickleball.

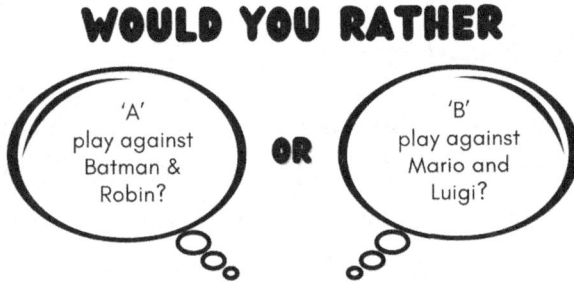

WOULD YOU RATHER

'A'
play against
Batman &
Robin?

OR

'B'
play against
Mario and
Luigi?

PROMOTING FUN AND RESPECT

Balancing Competition and Enjoyment

Picture yourself at the playground. Kids racing each other to the swings, with laughter and shouts filling the air—the thrill of the game balanced with the sheer fun of play. That's the spirit we need to bring to the pickleball court.

While it's natural to get caught up in the competitive aspect of pickleball, it's important to remember why we play in the first place—for the joy of it. The challenge lies in balancing the drive to win with the pure fun of playing the game.

It's about celebrating a well-executed shot, even if it doesn't score a point. It's about laughing off a miss, even if it costs you the game. It's about encouraging each other, learning together, and creating memories on the court. After all, pickleball is more than just a game; it's a source of fun, camaraderie, and enjoyment.

Fostering a Respectful Environment

Let's imagine you're at a picnic. Everyone's chatting, eating, and having a good time. There's a sense of mutual respect and an understanding of shared space. That's the kind of environment we want to foster on the pickleball court.

A respectful environment is one where every player feels valued, heard, and appreciated. It's an atmosphere that encourages learning, supports progress, and recognizes effort. It's a place where everyone adheres to the rules, respects the officials, and plays fair.

Creating such an environment starts with each one of us. It's about treating others how we'd like to be treated. It's about offering a helping hand, a kind word, and a genuine smile. It's about creating a space that's not just about playing pickleball but about being a part of the pickleball family.

Encouraging Inclusivity in Play

Think of a family dinner. Everyone's included, everyone's opinion matters, and everyone's part of the conversation. On the pickleball court, we strive for the same level of inclusivity.

Pickleball is a game for everyone—young and old, beginners and pros, casual players, and competitive athletes. It's a sport that doesn't discriminate but rather brings people together

Promoting inclusivity in play means welcoming all players, regardless of their skill level or experience. It's about creating opportunities for everyone to play, learn, and improve. It's about appreciating diversity, valuing individual strengths, and fostering a sense of belonging.

So, next time you step onto the court, remember to extend a warm welcome to everyone. After all, the beauty of pickleball lies not just in the game itself but in the vibrant, diverse, and inclusive community it creates.

As we wrap up this chapter, let's not forget that pickleball, at its heart, is more than just a sport. It's a celebration of community, an affirmation of respect, and a testament to the joy of play. It's a game that teaches us to balance competition and enjoyment, foster a respectful environment, and encourage inclusivity in play. As we step onto the court, paddle in hand, let's strive to uphold these values, to play with integrity, and to keep the spirit of this wonderful game alive. So, are you ready to serve up some fun, respect, and inclusivity on the pickleball court? Let's get to it!

Up next, we'll explore the thrill of competitive play, the exhilaration of tournaments, and the journey from being a beginner to becoming a seasoned player.

So, stay tuned, and let's keep this exciting pickleball adventure going! [1]

CELEBRITY *spotlight*

IN 2023, TYRA BLACK, AT THE AGE OF 22, JOINED THE MIAMI PICKLEBALL CLUB TEAM CO-OWNED BY SPORTS STARS PATRICK MAHOMES AND NAOMI OSAKA. HER PARENTS, NAMED HER TYRA 'HURRICANE' BLACK IN ANTICIPATION OF A TENNIS CAREER, WHILE HER SISTER, ALICIA, IS KNOWN AS 'TORNADO'. DESPITE HER TENNIS SUCCESS, TYRA WAS UNHAPPY IN THE SPORT AND MADE THE SWITCH TO PICKLEBALL. AS ONE OF THE FIRST BLACK WOMEN IN THE WORLD TO REACH THE TOP 10 IN PICKLEBALL, BLACK HOPES TO BRING MORE DIVERSITY TO THE SPORT. [34]

Tyra Black

CHAPTER 10

VENTURING INTO COMPETITIVE PLAY – THE FAMILY EDITION

L et's imagine it's a sunny Saturday; the smell of freshly cut grass is in the air, the sound of laughter echoes around, and the clinking sound of pickleball paddles fills the atmosphere. You see families—children, parents, grandparents—all geared up, their eyes sparkling with excitement and a tad bit of nervousness. Welcome to the world of competitive pickleball, where families don't just play together; they compete together.

Stepping into competitive play is like diving into a pool. The first dip might be a bit shocking, but once you're in, it's exhilarating. It's a space where fun meets focus, where learning meets competition, and where families bond over shared goals and friendly rivalry. So, let's dive in and explore how to prepare your family for this exciting plunge into competitive pickle ball!

PREPARING YOUR FAMILY FOR COMPETITIVE PLAY

Setting Realistic Expectations

Remember your child's first bike ride? They weren't popping wheelies or racing down the street on day one, were they? Much like learning to ride a bike, venturing into competitive pickleball requires setting realistic expectations.

DID YOU KNOW?

Player skill levels are rated from 1.0 (beginner) to 5.0 (professional).

It's important to understand that winning isn't the only goal. Yes, everyone loves to win, but in the early stages, focus on progress, not perfection. Celebrate the small victories—a well-executed serve, a successful volley, a match where everyone remembers the score! Set achievable goals for each family member and acknowledge every step forward, no matter how small.

Remember, pickleball is a game of skill that takes time to master. So, be patient, keep expectations realistic, and, most importantly, remember to have fun!

Developing a Training Schedule

Imagine preparing for a family camping trip. You'd plan your route, pack your equipment, and check the weather forecast, right? Training for competitive pickleball is similar; it requires planning and preparation.

Develop a training schedule that suits your family. Consider factors like work commitments, school schedules, and other activities. Aim for regular, short sessions rather than infrequent, long ones. Remember, consistency is key!

Your training sessions should focus on skill development, game strategy, and physical conditioning. Mix it up to keep it interesting. One day could be dedicated to serving and returning, another for dinks and volleys, and another for a friendly match to put those skills to the test.

Remember, the goal of training is not just to improve skills but also to foster teamwork and understanding among family members. After all, a family that plays together stays together!

Mental Preparation for Competitive Play

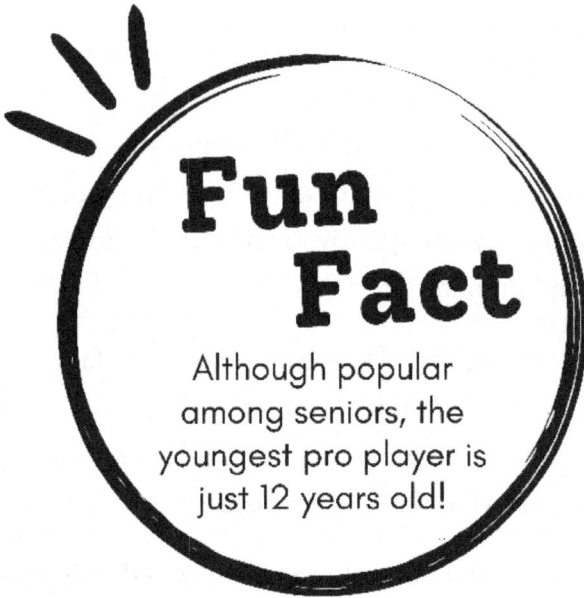

Fun Fact

Although popular among seniors, the youngest pro player is just 12 years old!

Picture yourself before an important presentation or meeting. You'd probably spend some time preparing mentally, calming your nerves, and focusing your thoughts, right? Mental preparation is as crucial in pickleball as it is in any other challenging situation.

Help your family understand that it's normal to feel nervous before a match. Share techniques to manage these pre-match jitters. This could be deep breathing exercises, visualization techniques, or simply listening to some calming music.

Encourage a positive mindset. Remind each other that it's okay to miss a shot, it's okay to lose a point, and it's okay to make mistakes. What matters is to keep trying, keep learning, and keep enjoying the game.

Remember, the mind is a powerful tool. A well-prepared mind can be your secret weapon in competitive play. So, gear up, tune in, and get your game face on!

As we step into the world of competitive pickleball, it's important to remember that it's more than just a game. It's an opportunity to learn, to grow, and to bond as a family. It's about the thrill of the match, the cheers on a well-earned point, and the high-fives exchanged—win or lose. So, grab your paddles, gather your team, and let's make a splash in the exciting pool of competitive pickleball!

UNDERSTANDING SKILL LEVELS AND RATINGS

Pickleball enthusiasts are evaluated according to their proficiency in the game. This evaluation is represented numerically and is commonly known as a pickleball rating, often interchangeable with the term pickleball skill level. There are a few systems used to rate or rank your pickleball skills on the pickleball court, which include:

- Self-Rating
- USA Pickleball Tournament Player Rating (UTPR)
- Dynamic Universal Pickleball Ratings (DUPR)

Self-Rating

Pickleball enthusiasts have the option to assign themselves a self-rating, aptly named as such. Self-ratings consist of two digits (e.g., 3.0, 3.5, 4.0, etc.). Any pickleball player, regardless of tournament participation or USA Pickleball membership, can assign themselves a two-digit self-rating based on the following guidelines:

Beginner (1.0 to 2.4)

(1.0): The player is new to pickleball with limited knowledge of the game's rules and terminology.

(1.5): The player can hit the ball back and forth, is learning to serve, fails to hit easy balls frequently, and is beginning to learn scoring and basic rules.

(2.0): The player has limited experience but can sustain a short rally with players of equal ability, can keep score, and is starting to understand court positioning and doubles rules.

Novice (2.5 to 3.4)

(2.5): The player can sustain longer rallies but not at a fast pace, is starting to make most easy shots frequently, and has a good understanding of rules but still struggles to cover the entire court.

(3.0): The player consistently serves and returns in bounds, is starting to play at a medium pace, lacks control when trying to place the ball, and attempts lobs and dinks with limited success.

Intermediate (3.5 to 3.9):

(3.5): The player has consistent control and placement of medium-placed shots, is able to return fast-paced shots, has improved control and placement of the ball, can play aggressively at the non-volley line, and is starting to anticipate the opponent's shots.

Advanced (4.0 to 4.9):

(4.0): The player is consistent with all strokes, is starting to use spin with some success, uses the dink and drop shot successfully, demonstrates 3rd shot strategies, plays aggressively at the non-volley line, and has a full understanding of the rules.

(4.5): The player is masting placement and spin with some frequency, has good footwork and positioning, adjusts his/her playing style to opponents' weaknesses, has good court positioning, and anticipates opponents' shots.

Expert/Pro (5.0+):

(5.0): The player has mastered all shot types, strategies, and positioning and varies the pace of play.

Visit the USA Pickleball webpage for a detailed description of each skill level.

USA Pickleball Tournament Player Rating (UTPR)

USA Pickleball and PickleballTournaments.com, a tournament software company, calculates player ratings based on tournament win/loss results and opponents' UTPR for USA Pickleball-sanctioned events. The rating system is based on the same 1.0–5.0 rating system as described above for self-ranking.

Visit the USA Pickleball UTPR webpage for a detail description.

Dynamic Universal Pickleball Ratings (DUPR)

Dynamic Universal Pickleball Rating is the most accurate and only global rating system in pickle ball. All players, regardless of their age, gender, location, or skill, are rated on the same scale between 2.0–8.0 based on their match result.

Visit myDUPR for a detailed description of each skill level and to create a DUPR account.

UNDERSTANDING TOURNAMENT RULES

Picture yourself preparing for a fun-filled road trip. You'd probably start by looking at the route, checking the must-see spots along the way, and planning your breaks. Just as you'd familiarize yourself with the route to make your road trip smoother, understanding the structure of the tournament can help you navigate the competitive pickleball journey with ease.

Pickleball tournaments typically feature the following event categories:

- Men's – Singles and Doubles
- Women's – Singles and Doubles
- Mixed – Doubles

For participation in men's or women's events, only individuals of the respective gender are eligible to compete. In mixed doubles events, one partner must be male, and the other partner must be female.

When a doubles team is categorized by age and/or skill level, the partner with the younger age determines the age group in which the team will compete. For example, if a 19-year-old plays with a 60-year-old, the doubles team will compete in the 19+ age division. Similarly, the partner with the higher skill level dictates the skill level division in which the team will compete. For instance, if a 5.0 player plays with a 3.5 player, the doubles team will compete in the 5.0+ division.

In the absence of a junior division, any player who is 18 years old or younger and wishes to participate in a pickleball tournament may enter the 19+ age division.

Every tournament has its own unique structure, dictated by factors such as the number of participating teams, the duration of the tournament, and the specific rules of the organizing body. It could be a round-robin format where every team plays all other teams, a knockout format where a single defeat sends you packing, or a combination of both pickleball tournament formats.

Pickleball tournaments employ various formats for competition, each with its unique rules. These may include:

- **Round Robin:** In a round-robin format, all players/teams compete against each other, and the winning player/team is determined by win-loss records. Ties are resolved first by head-to-head matches, then by point differential, and, if necessary, by head-to-head point differential. If a tie still persists, the final tiebreaker is based on a point differential against the next-highest team.

- **Single Elimination:** In this format, players or teams are eliminated after a loss.
- **Double Elimination:** In this format, once a team loses, they move to the "consolation bracket" and begin competing for bronze. Gold/silver or first/second place is exclusively contested among players/teams remaining in the winner's bracket
- **Pool Play:** Pool play operates similarly to round robin, with players/teams within a pool playing against each other. Based on pool play results, teams are seeded into either a single-elimination or double-elimination bracket.

Regardless of the format used, all pickleball tournaments usually guarantee participants play a minimum number of games.

Remember, knowledge is power. By understanding the tournament structure, you'll be better prepared to face the challenges that come your way.

Get a hold of the tournament schedule beforehand. Know who you're playing, when you're playing, and on which court. This will not only help you plan your games but also allow you to study your opponents in advance.

Adapting to Different Tournament Formats

Imagine you're an actor who's been performing in a comedy play, and suddenly, you're cast in a drama. You'd have to adapt your acting style to suit the new genre, right? Similarly, in pickleball, you may need to adapt your game strategy to suit different tournament formats.

Some tournaments might be singles, others doubles or mixed doubles. Some might be age-based, others skill-based. Each format calls for a different approach, a different strategy, and a different mindset.

In singles, for instance, you're the lone warrior. You've got the entire court to cover but also the freedom to play every shot. In doubles, on the other hand, teamwork comes into play. You need to coordinate with your partner, cover your respective courts, and set up shots for each other.

Being flexible and adaptable is key. Be ready to change your game strategy, tweak your techniques, and step out of your comfort zone. After all, pickleball is as much about adaptability as it is about skill.

Preparing for Rule Variations

Think about the last time you played a board game with friends. Did you stick to the official rules, or did you introduce some fun variations of your own? Just like those board game nights, pickleball tournaments can have variations in rules.

While the basic rules of pickleball remain the same, tournaments often introduce slight variations to add a unique flavor. For instance, some tournaments might use the Coman Tiebreak method in case of a tie; others might stick to the traditional tiebreaker. Some might have specific rules for service orders or player positions in doubles.

Stay updated with these variations. Read through the tournament rulebook, attend the pre-tournament briefing, and, when in doubt, don't hesitate to ask the officials for clarification.

Being prepared for rule variations will not only keep you from unpleasant surprises but also give you an edge over less-prepared opponents. So, roll up your sleeves, brush up your rulebook, and get ready to play by the rules, whatever they may be!

There you go! You're now equipped with insights into the structure and format of tournaments, as well as an understanding of how to handle rule variations. As you gear up for your foray into competitive pickleball, remember that every tournament is a new adventure, every match a new challenge, and every point a step closer to your goal. So, pack your gear, rally your spirits, and get set for an exhilarating ride into the world of competitive pickleball.

Check out First Tournament Tips by Sarah Ansboury on YouTube.

How does a pickleball player show affection?

HA HA HA

They give you a little "dink!"

The USA Pickleball official rulebook is available for download on their website.[1]

STRATEGIES FOR COMPETITIVE MATCHES

Analyzing Opponent's Play Style

Imagine you're a detective, diligently observing, picking up clues, and making deductions. In the realm of competitive pickleball, adopting this detective mindset can give you a significant edge in the game.

Before the match, take some time to study your opponents. Do they favor a strong serve or a strategic one? Are they aggressive players who prefer smashing, or are they masters of the delicate dink? Do they stick to a particular pattern, or are they unpredictable in their gameplay? These clues about their play style can help you formulate an effective strategy.

Remember, in the grand scheme of pickleball, knowledge is power. The more you know about your opponents' play style, the better prepared you'll be to counter their moves and make your own.

Adapting Strategy Mid-Game

Consider the ever-changing colors of a chameleon. Just as this remarkable creature adapts to its surroundings, being flexible and adaptable with your game strategy is crucial in competitive pickleball.

A game of pickleball is dynamic and fluid. What works in one game might not work in another. Even within the same game, the effectiveness of a strategy can change as the game progresses. Perhaps your opponents have found a way to counter your powerful serves, or your excellent dinking strategy is being neutralized by their impressive volleys.

In such situations, being able to adapt your strategy mid-game can make the difference between victory and defeat. It could mean switching from an aggressive play to a more strategic one, changing your serving style, or even repositioning yourself on the court.

Remember, in pickleball, as in life, the ability to adapt is key. So, stay flexible, stay open, and be ready to switch strategies when needed.

WOW

The total prize pool of pickleball tournaments is estimated at $10M in 2023[40]

Importance of Warm-Up and Cool-Down

Imagine you're about to run a marathon. Would you just jump off the couch and start running? Probably not. You'd stretch, warm up your muscles, and get your heart rate up, right? The same principle applies to pickleball.

While it's easy to overlook in the excitement of a match, a good warm-up is crucial to prepare your body for the physical demands of the game. It can enhance your performance, increase your flexibility, and reduce the risk of injuries. Your warm-up could include light cardio, some dynamic stretching, and a few practice shots with the paddle.

Similarly, after the match, a cool-down session is essential to bring your heart rate down, relax your muscles, and speed up recovery. Gentle stretching, slow-paced walking, and deep breathing exercises are effective cool-down activities.

So, whether you're gearing up for a match or winding down after one, remember the importance of a good warm-up and cool-down. It's not just about playing better; it's about playing smarter and safer. So, stretch, warm up, play, cool down, and repeat. That's the mantra for a healthy, successful pickleball experience.

WOULD YOU RATHER

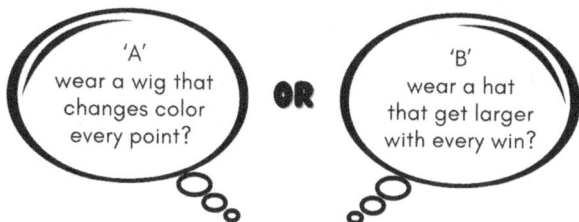

'A'
wear a wig that
changes color
every point?

OR

'B'
wear a hat
that get larger
with every win?

CELEBRATING SUCCESS AND HANDLING DEFEAT

Recognizing Effort over Outcome

Think about a time when you baked a cake for the first time. Did you focus on how it tasted, or were you more excited about the fact that you baked it yourself? Similar is the scenario when you step into the realm of competitive pickleball. The outcome of the match, while thrilling, shouldn't overshadow the efforts made.

Highlight the progress your family has made over time. Did someone master that tricky serve? Did the kids manage to keep their cool throughout a challenging match? As a family, it's important to value these small victories. They are the stepping stones to becoming not just better players but a stronger team.

So, let's put on our metaphorical chef hats and appreciate the process, the effort, and the teamwork. After all, every pickleball match is a recipe for hard work, determination, and a whole lot of fun!

Reflecting on Performance Post-Match

Have you ever watched a movie and discussed it with friends afterward? You talk about the plot, the characters, your favorite scenes, what worked, and what didn't. Post-match reflection in pickleball is quite similar. It's an opportunity to analyze your performance, understand what went well, and identify areas for improvement.

After a match, gather your family and discuss the game. What were the standout moments? What strategies worked? Where did you face challenges? This open dialogue can provide valuable insights on how to improve for future games.

Remember, every game is a learning experience. So, consider each match as a new episode in your pickleball adventure, and don't forget to discuss the highlights after the credits roll.

Using Defeat as Motivation for Improvement

Picture yourself trying to solve a complex puzzle. You hit dead ends and make the wrong moves, but you don't give up. You learn from your mistakes, adjust your strategy, and keep going until you solve them. Handling defeat in pickleball is a similar process.

Losing a match can be disappointing, but it can also fuel your determination to improve. It shines a spotlight on areas that need work and provides a clear direction for your practice sessions. That missed volley or unsuccessful serve is not a failure but feedback on what to work on next.

So, the next time you face defeat, don't let it dampen your spirits. Instead, let it ignite your determination to grow stronger and play better. After all, in the grand game of pickleball, defeat is just a stepping stone on the path to success.

And with that, we wrap up our deep dive into the fascinating world of competitive pickleball. Remember, every serve, every shot, and every point is part of the incredible adventure that is pickleball. So, keep practicing, keep playing, and keep enjoying this wonderful sport.

As we gear up for the next chapter, let's continue to celebrate the joy, the challenges, and the camaraderie of pickleball. Because whether you're playing a friendly match in your backyard or competing in a tournament, pickleball is more than just a sport—it's a way of life. So, grab your paddles, gather your team, and let's keep the ball rolling! Onward to the next chapter of our pickleball adventure! [2]

Hayden Patriquin

CELEBRITY *spotlight*

HAYDEN PATRIQUIN IS ONE OF THE SPORT'S YOUNGEST PLAYERS MAKING HIS PROFESSIONAL DEBUT IN 2022 AT THE AGE OF 16. LATER THAT YEAR, HE SECURED A REMARKABLE VICTORY AGAINST RAFA HEWETT, A TOP-20 WORLD PICKLEBALL RANKED PLAYER, DURING THE 2022 APP MESA OPEN. HAYDEN WAS INTRODUCED TO THE SPORT AT THE AGE OF 12 BY HIS GRANDFATHER. [41]

SHARE THE NEWS ABOUT PICKLEBALL!

As you come to the end of this book, my hope is that you've already played a few matches and maybe even found a local pickleball league so you and your family can enjoy the thrill of competitive friendly play. The fun only grows when more people sign up, and I hope you can do your share by letting other readers know how accessible, fun, and affordable this game is.

Now that you know the regulations, strategies, and techniques of pickleball, there's one thing left to say... see you and your family on the court this weekend! Here's to many days of fast-paced fun in the presence of those you love!

Scan the QR code below

CONCLUSION: THE LAST ACE IN THE PICKLEBALL PADDLE BAG

As we stand here, paddles down with glistening foreheads, catching our breath, we can't help but look back at the exhilarating pickleball journey we've had together. We've laughed, we've stumbled, we've served, and we've volleyed. We've turned from pickleball novices into pickleball aficionados—all in the course of a few chapters.

We've discovered that pickleball is more than just a sport; it's a social phenomenon, a family bonding experience, and a secret remedy for Monday blues. We've learned the art of the serve, the thrill of the volley, and the magic of the dink. We've embraced defeat, celebrated victories, and turned the pickleball court into our own personal comedy club.

Looking ahead, the future of pickleball appears as bright as a shiny new pickleball paddle under the summer sun. The sport is growing, the community is expanding, and the opportunities to play are multiplying faster than you can say "pickleball" five times in a row. So, keep the ball rolling, my friends. The pickleball adventure has just begun.

But why keep all the fun to ourselves? Let's spread the pickleball bug far and wide. Encourage your friends to join the pickleball parade. Invite your neighbors for a friendly match. Teach your grandkids the joys of the dink shot. Show your pet turtle that there's more to life than lettuce (though I doubt he'll be able to hold a paddle, let alone serve).

In the end, remember, pickleball isn't just about hitting a whiffle ball with a paddle. It's about laughter, camaraderie, and a sense of belonging. It's about shared experiences, friendly competition, and the simple joy of play. It's about families coming together, communities growing stronger, and life becoming a little more fun.

So, as we wrap up this pickleball saga, here's my final serve to you: keep playing, keep laughing, and keep loving pickleball. Because at the end of the day, it's not about how well you served or how many games you won. It's about the smiles you shared, the friends you made, and the love for the game you kindled.

Thank you for joining me on this pickleball adventure. Keep the paddles swinging, the balls flying, and the laughter echoing on the court. Until next time, my fellow pickleball enthusiasts, may your serves be swift, your volleys victorious, and your dinks delightful. Now, go forth and pickleball!

GLOSSARY

Ace: A serve not returned by the opponent.

Alley: The extension of the court by 1.5 feet on both sides used only in doubles play.

Angle Shot: A ball hit with a sharp angle, aiming to go wide of the opponent.

Approach Shot: An aggressive shot hit while advancing towards the net.

Attack: Aggressive play or shots aimed at winning the point.

B

Backcourt: The last few feet of the back of the court nearest the baseline that is still within the court boundaries.

Backhand: A stroke hit with the back of the paddle facing the net.

Backspin: Spin where the ball rotates backwards as it travels.

Baseline: The line marking the back boundary of the court.

Banger: A player using the slammers playstyle where the ball is hit hard and fast repeatedly.

Block: A defensive shot placing the paddle in the path of a powerful ball.

Bump: A ball hit with pace but without spin.

C

Carry: A fault where the ball is caught and carried on the paddle.

Centerline: The painted line that runs down the middle of the court, diving it into two halves, is the centerline. It runs from the baseline to the non-volley line.

Chip Shot: A low trajectory shot created by hitting the ball with backspin.

Continental Grip: A grip where the base knuckle of the index finger is on the second bevel of the paddle.

Cross-Court: A shot directed diagonally across the court.

Cut Shot: A ball hit with underspin, causing it to drop quickly and skid.

D

Dink: A soft, controlled shot aiming to land in the non-volley zone.

Deep Serve: A serve that lands in the far back region of the opponent's court.

Double Bounce Rule: Each team must let the ball bounce once before hitting it after the serve.

Double Elimination: A tournament format where a team or player is eliminated after two losses.

Doubles: A match format where two players play against two players.

Drive: A fast, flat shot aimed at pushing the opponent backward.

Drop Shot: A soft shot aimed at landing just over the net in the non-volley zone.

E

Erne: A volley hit after stepping into the non-volley zone to counter soft shots.

Energy Transfer: The transfer of energy from the paddle to the ball influencing speed and spin.

Engagement Rule: A player cannot cross into the non-volley zone until their shot has passed the net.

Exhibition Match: A non-competitive game showcasing skilled players.

F

Fault: A rule violation leading to the loss of the serve or a point.

Foot Fault: A violation where a player steps into the non-volley zone while volleying.

Follow-Through: The continuation of motion after the ball is struck.

Forced Error: An error induced by the opponent's skillful play.

Forehand: A shot made with the front of the paddle facing the net.

G

Game Point: The point that, if won by the server, wins the game.

Groundstroke: A shot hit after the ball has bounced.

Grip: The manner in which players hold the paddle.

H

Half-Volley: A shot hit immediately after the ball bounces.

Head Fake: Deceiving opponents about shot direction using head movement.

Hinder: An obstruction that affects the outcome of a point, leading to a replay.

J

Joust: Both players contacting the ball above the net at the same time.

Jump Smash: A powerful overhead shot hit while jumping.

K

Kitchen: Another term for the non-volley zone.

Kitchen Line: The line that separated the non-volley zone from the mid-court.

L

Let Serve: A serve that touches the net but lands in, leading to a re-serve.

Line Call: A decision by a player or official if a shot is in or out.

Lob: A high-arcing shot sending the opponent back to the baseline.

Lunge: A large step to extend reach during play.

M

Match Point: A point that, if won, concludes the match.

Midcourt: The middle area of the court between baseline and net.

Mixed Doubles: A team of one male and one female player.

N

Net Height: The regulated height of the net at the center of the net and at the net posts.

Net Play: Action close to the net involving volleys and dinks.

No Mans Land: A slang term for the midcourt.

Non-Volley Zone (NVZ): A 7-foot area from the net where volleying is not allowed.

O

Out Ball: A ball landing outside the court boundaries.

Overhead Smash: A powerful shot hit from above the player's head.

P

Paddle Face: The hitting surface of the paddle.

Passing Shot: A shot aimed to pass the opponent without them hitting it.

Placement: Targeting shots to exploit opponent's weaknesses.

Poach: Moving to hit a ball in partner's area of the court.

Punch Volley: A quick, controlled volley with minimal backswing.

Put Away: A shot that is executed with enough speed, precision, or placement that the opponent cannot return.

Q

Quick Serve: Rapidly executed serve to catch the opponent off-guard.

Quality Shot: A well-executed shot making it difficult for opponents to return.

R

Rally: Continuous exchange of shots between players or teams.

Ready Position: The stance players adopt while awaiting the opponent's shot.

Red Zone: The critical area near the net where players need to be alert.

Referee: Official ensuring the match adheres to the rules.

Replay: The repetition of a point after an interruption or a let.

Return of Serve: A shot hit by the receiving team following the serve.

S

Serve: The stroke initiating play, hit diagonally into opponent's service court.

Serve Number: In doubles games, it is mandatory for the server to call the server number "1" or "2" prior to serving. The number depends on whether you were the first or second server on your side.

Shadowing: Moving in sync with your doubles partner during a game.

Side Out: The term "side out" means that the serving side is "out" of turns to serve, and the serve switches to the other team or player. The term originated in volleyball and has been adopted in pickleball.

Sideline: The outer lines on each side of the court that run from the net to the baseline.

Sidespin: Spin where the ball rotates around its vertical axis.

Singles: A match format where one player competes against another.

Skinny Singles: A math format similar to singles but played on a half court on one side of the centerline.

Slammers: A playstyle where the ball is hit hard and fast repeatedly.

Slice: Striking the ball with a chopping, downward motion resulting in underspin on the ball.

Smash: A hard, overhead shot.

Stacking: A strategy in doubles play to keep the stronger player on one side.

Strategy: A planned approach to outplay the opponent.

Stroke: The action of hitting the ball with the paddle.

Spin: The ball's rotation affecting its flight and bounce.

T

Third Shot Drop: A soft shot following the serve and return, aimed at NVZ.

Topspin: Forward spin causing the ball to dip and bounce higher.

Transition Zone: The area players pass through moving to the net.

Tweener: A shot that is hit between the legs.

U

Unforced Error: A mistake made during easy play, leading to point loss.

Underhand Serve: A serve hit below the waist in an upward motion.

Upset: Lower-ranked player or team defeating a higher-ranked opponent.

V

Volley: Striking the ball before it hits the ground.

Volley Exchange: Rapid exchange of volleys, often near the net.

W

Windshield Wiper: Forehand or backhand motion resembling a car's wipers.

Wrong-Footing: Hitting the ball where the opponent has just vacated.

X

X-Factor: Unpredictable element influencing the match outcome.

Y

Yips: Nervousness causing unsteady play or missed shots.

Z

Zero-Zero-Start: The call starting the game, indicating a 0-0 score and first serve.

Zone Serving: Targeting specific areas during the serve to exploit opponent's weakness.

REFERENCES

Here are the references in alphabetical order:

"Athlete Anna Leigh Waters." Accessed July 2023. http://www.ppatour.com/athlete/anna-leigh-waters/.

Ben Johns. "What's in My Bag." YouTube Video. Accessed July 2023. https://www.youtube.com/watch?v=-1_I5fKoQgU.

Better Pickleball. "Pickleball Scoring Basics – Make it Easy with Me, You and Who?" YouTube Video. Accessed July 2023. https://youtu.be/eMEpFipIdrk?si=edZl4nRIwIC-ZUgO.

CBS News. "Pickleball professional sport: How much you can earn?" Accessed October 2023. https://www.cbsnews.com/news/pickleball-professional-sport-how-much-you-can-earn/.

Chronicles_of_IMan. Instagram profile. Accessed September 2023. https://www.instagram.com/Chronicles_of_IMan.

Cincola, John. Court Positioning Fundamentals: You Can't Play Great Pickleball Unless You're in the Right Spot. YouTube Video. Accessed September 2023. https://youtu.be/5R6oYi7nUt8?si=FRXAyKAxs7CXG4OB.

DUPR Pickleball. Accessed September 2023. https://mydupr.com/.

ESPN. "Kevin Durant latest sports star to own pickleball franchise." Accessed September 2023. https://www.espn.com/nba/story/_/id/34838548/kevin-durant-latest-sports-star-own-pickleball-franchise.

Gamble, Casey. "30+ Pickleball Quotes & Captions That Prove Why It's Awesome." Love to Know. August 2, 2023. https://www.lovetoknow.com/quotes-quips/daily-life/pickleball-quotes-captions

Gates, Bill. "Fifty years ago, I started playing this little-known sport with a funny name. Now, it's all the rage." GateNotes. Blog post, July 26, 2022.

Guinness World Records. "Longest Pickleball Rally." Accessed September 2023. https://www.guinnessworldrecords.com/world-records/669898-longest-pickleball-rally.

Holderness Family. "The 5 Stages of Pickleball." YouTube Video. Accessed July 2023. https://youtu.be/tYX5l6jsoiU?si=29iikvl7hPvYO6x7.

Holderness Family Music. If Pearl Jam Explained Pickleball Rules. YouTube

Video. Accessed October 2023. https://youtube.com/shorts/iHDq53ZqBzk?si=fJGlkaan_ryoS9Xk.

Holderness Family Music. Ode to Pickleball - "Wrecking Ball" Parody. YouTube Video. Accessed October 2023. https://www.youtube.com/watch?v=95_He EELzYU.

Holderness Family Music. Pickleball Symphony. YouTube Video. Accessed October 2023. https://www.youtube.com/watch?v=oQhPA9irWPk.

Holderness Family Music. The Pickleball Song. YouTube Video. Accessed October 2023. https://www.youtube.com/watch?v=MtEWJSc_FJw.

International Pickleball Federation. "About the International Pickleball Federation." Accessed August 2023. https://theipf.org/about.html.

Johns, Ben. The Keys to Gaining Mental Strength on the Pickleball Court. YouTube Video. Accessed September 2023. https://youtu.be/oCvDxodJESQ?si=cMKlcMI47EwI34hO.

Kim Kardashian Plays Pickleball. Facebook Video. Accessed July 2023. https://fb.watch/nuBvGItP9f/.

Major League Pickleball. "Hayden Patriquin." Accessed October 2023. https://www.majorleaguepickleball.net/player/hayden-patriquin/.

Major League Pickleball. "Premier League." Accessed October 2023. https://www.majorleaguepickleball.net/premier-league/.

Pickleball Channel. "5 Steps to a Winning Dink. Video. Accessed July 2023. https://www.pickleballchannel.com/PB411-Dinking-101.

Pickleball Channel. "Non-Volley Rule Explained." Accessed July 2023. https://www.pickleballchannel.com/PB411-NVZ-Rule.

Pickleball Channel. "The Underhand Serve." Accessed July 2023. https://www.pickleballchannel.com/pickleball-411-the-underhand-serve/.

"Pickleball Channel." Non-Volley Rule Explained. YouTube Video. Accessed July 2023. https://www.pickleballchannel.com/PB411-NVZ-Rule.

"Pickleball Channel." The Underhand Serve. YouTube Video. Accessed July 2023. https://www.pickleballchannel.com/pickleball-411-the-underhand-serve/.

"Pickleball Channel." Three Serves and Why You Need Them. YouTube Video. Accessed July 2023. https://www.pickleballchannel.com/pickleball-411-three-serves-and-why-you-need-them/.

Pickleball for the Cure. Accessed September 2023. https://pickleballforthecure.donordrive.com/index.cfm?fuseaction=cms.home.

Pickleball Guy, The. 3rd Shot Drop vs. Drive: Which to use and WHEN?

YouTube Video. Accessed September 2023. https://youtu.be/LnTAm5pAr9c?si=oUGyob6S1yW77mqY.

Pickleball Guy, The. 6 Pickleball Doubles Strategies New Players MUST Know. YouTube Video. Accessed September 2023. https://www.youtube.com/watch?v=JGMLn68RZS8.

Pickleball Guy, The. How to Serve: A Beginner's Guide. YouTube Video. Accessed September 2023. https://youtu.be/BmdnJNCEwxI?si=m2MwFY5W_nVHCjmL.

Pickleball Guy, The. "7 Kitchen Strategies to Avoid Getting Crushed in Pickleball." YouTube Video. Accessed July 2023. https://youtu.be/JxVFdb1PixU?si=-XHkzNPVRSUwUAt9.

Pickleball Magazine. "'Hurricane' Tyra Black Takes Pickleball by Storm." Accessed October 2023. https://www.pickleballmagazine.com/cover

Pickleball Magazine. Pickleball Quick Tip: How to Hit a Better Return of Serve. YouTube Video. Accessed July 2023. https://youtu.be/cX-nyshUCQQ?si=_vJKhEdhMxPDooq6.

"Paddle Guide." Pickleball Central. Accessed August 2023. https://www.pickleballcentral.com.

PrimeTime Pickleball. Deep Serves and Returns. YouTube Video. Accessed September 2023. https://www.youtube.com/watch?v=nKQU52FB_2s.

PrimeTime Pickleball. Slow Motion Serves with Top Players. YouTube Video. Accessed September 202

APPENDIX A – WHO'S WHO OF PICKLEBALL

Here are just a few of the names you should know in the world of pickleball.

Anna Leigh Waters – at only 16 years old and as of October 2022, she is ranked No. 1 in the world for doubles, No. 1 for mixed doubles, and No. 1 for singles by the Professional Pickleball Association.

Ben Johns - Currently the #1 ranked men's singles player. Known for his power and athleticism.

Simone Jardim - Top-ranked woman player who won gold at the 2021 World Pickleball Championships.

Tyson McGuffin - #1 ranked men's doubles player. Excellent volleys and quickness at the net.

Catherine Parenteau - Legendary player inducted into the Pickleball Hall of Fame in 2021. Won over 50 gold medals.

Jennifer Dawson - Won 3 gold medals at the 2021 World Pickleball Championships. Former tennis pro.

Riley Newman - Rising young star, won U18 singles title at 2022 National Championships at age 15.

Lea Jansen - Won the 2022 National Senior Games at age 85! Ambassador for seniors playing pickleball.

Visit Major League Pickleball for a list of professional players and team owners.[1] You'll be surprised at how household names, celebrities and professional athletes alike, own pickleball teams.

APPENDIX B - 50 PICKLEBALL JOKES FOR THE WHOLE FAMILY

Pickleball

1. Why was the pickleball court so hot? Because all the fans left early!
2. Why do pickleball players always bring an extra pair of socks? In case they get a foot fault!
3. Why was the pickleball player like a musician? Because every hit was a smash hit!
4. How do pickleball players stay cool? They sit next to their fans!
5. Why did the pickle turn down dessert? It was already stuffed to the dill!
6. Why did the pickle lose the tournament? It couldn't cut the mustard!
7. Why did the pickleball team go to the bank? To get their bounce checked!
8. How does a pickle answer the phone? "Yellow?"

9. Why do pickleball players make great detectives? They know how to bounce ideas back and forth!

10. What's a pickleball player's favorite type of music? Anything with a good bounce!

11. What do you call a pickle who's an expert at trick shots? A con-dill-ment artist!

12. Why did the ball get expelled from pickleball school? For being a little dill-inquent!

13. Why was the pickleball court so loud? Because all the balls were having a smashing time!

14. Why did the pickleball player bring a ladder to the game? To climb the rankings!

15. How do pickleball players stay in touch? They always keep in service!

16. Why did the pickleball player fart during the serve? They were under a lot of pressure!

17. Why was the referee give the pickle a penalty? For excessive dill-lay of game!

18. How do pickleball players keep their skin smooth? With a good backspin!

19. Why did the pickleball player bring string to the game? To tie the score!

20. Why did the pickleball player join a band? Because they had great timing!

21. What do you call a pickleball tournament for spies? A secret dill service!

22. What did one pickle say to the other during a game? "Let's bounce back from this loss and dill with it!"

23. What do pickleball players wear to bed? Their net-gowns!

24. Why don't pickleball players tell secrets on the court? Because of all the net working!

25. What's the pickle's favorite dance? The dill-y dally!

26. Why did the scarecrow win a pickleball trophy? Because he was outstanding in his field!

27. What's a pickleball player's favorite candy? Lifesavers, for those close calls!

28. What's the biggest lie in pickleball? "Just one more game!"

29. How do you make a pickleball dance? Serve it a good spin!

30. Why don't ghosts play pickleball? They can never get a body on the court!

31. Why did the pickle bring a ladder to the game? It wanted to take its skills to the next level!

32. Why did the pickleball player bring a pencil? To draw a line on those close calls!

33. How do pickleball players show affection? They give you a little "dink!"

34. How do pickleball players like their eggs? Well-volleyed!

35. What did the pickleball player say to the faulty net? "You need to pull yourself together!"

36. Why did the pickleball player become a baker? They were great at slicing!

37. Why don't skeletons fight each other on the pickleball court? They don't have the guts!

38. How do pickleball players say goodbye? It's been a smashing time!

39. What is a pickleball player's favorite song? Hit me with your best shot!

40. How do pickleball players keep their energy up during a match? With paddle-aid!

41. Why did the vampire refuse to play pickleball? He couldn't stand the stakes!

42. Why don't oysters donate to pickleball charity events? Because they are shellfish!

43. How do you make a tissue dance at a pickleball game? Put a little boogie in it!

44. Why did the pickleball player put his money in the blender? Because he wanted liquid assets!

45. Why is the pickleball team so good at parties? Because they really knew how to "smash"!

46. Why was the pickleball book such a thrilling read? Because it had a lot of "top spins"!

47. What do you serve but never eat? A pickleball!

48. Why was the computer so good at pickleball? Because it had a hard drive!

49. How do you know when you've played too much pickleball? When you try to serve the dinner!

50. Why are fish so bad at pickleball? They don't like getting close to the net!

APPENDIX C – 75 PICKLEBALL WOULD YOU RATHER QUESTIONS

1. Would you rather be an amazing server or have incredible reflexes at the net?
2. Would you rather be a doubles specialist or a stellar singles player?
3. Would you rather be able to place your serves perfectly or smash lightning-fast returns?
4. Would you rather win a medal at nationals or coach kids at the community center?
5. Would you rather have the best backhand shot or the most deceptive drop shot?
6. Would you rather have a fabulous backyard pickleball court or unlimited pro shop access?
7. Would you rather have the chance to play pickleball with LeBron James or Serena Williams?
8. Would you rather be able to read your opponent's moves before they happen or have endless stamina?

9. Would you rather be interviewed as a pickleball pro on ESPN or have your skills go viral on YouTube?

10. Would you rather be known for your "pickleball trash talk" or be the most polite player on the court?

11. Would you rather only be able to communicate in sports puns during a game or have to shout "Pickle!" every time you hit the ball?

12. Would you rather have a spectacular diving save or pull off a "tweener" winner between your legs?

13. Would you rather have amazing reflexes and speed or the most accurate lob shots?

14. Would you rather win gold at the Pickleball National Championships or $10,000?

15. Would you rather design your own custom paddles or exclusive pickleball clothing line?

16. Would you rather be able to play like the top 5 pickleball pros combined or travel the world playing pickleball?

17. Would you rather play a game where every point scored changes the rules slightly or where the net height randomly adjusts?

18. Would you rather be able to read spins perfectly or be able to place your serve exactly where you want?

19. Would you rather face off against aliens or medieval knights?

20. Would you rather be known for your amazing reflexes or your Zen-like patience and discipline?

21. Would you rather have a fantastic comeback win from a huge deficit or a flawless victory shutting out your opponent?

22. Would you rather every win turns the court a new color or every loss makes the court shrink?

23. Would you rather have the fancy trophy or a long celebratory feast after the tournament?

24. Would you rather get to rename the "kitchen" zone or create a new required warm-up ritual?

25. Would you rather have a signature move named after you or a new style of paddle crafted for you?

26. Would you rather face an opponent who sings badly while playing or one who tells terrible dad jokes every time they score?

27. Would you rather be a top doubles team with your best friend or have an epic singles rivalry?

28. Would you rather wear a wig that changes color every point or wear a hat that gets larger with every win?

29. Would you rather play against Batman and Robin or play against Mario and Luigi?

30. Would you rather win and get a cake smashed in your face or win and eat a jar of pickles?

31. Would you rather play pickleball for fun or play pickleball for competition?

32. Would you rather have a match narrated live by a famous comedian or have a world-renowned musician play live music during your game?

33. Would you rather have the ability to play pickleball in zero gravity or play on a court that's holographically projected in exotic locations?

34. Would you rather play a match where every shot is in slow motion or where your paddles change size randomly?

35. Would you rather train with a world champion or have a world-class facility to practice in?

36. Would you rather play in extreme heat or extreme cold?

37. Would you rather play against a much weaker opponent or a much stronger opponent?

38. Would you rather play against invisible opponents or ones that can't stop giggling?

39. Would you rather have a cheering crowd or complete silence during your matches?

40. Would you rather play a game that lasts an hour or a game that lasts 5 minutes?

41. Would you rather have a professional coach or self-taught skills?

42. Would you rather play pickleball every day or only once a week?

43. Would you rather always play with a new ball or with a worn-in ball?

44. Would you rather play in a team with great chemistry but less skill or a team with high skill but no chemistry?

45. Would you rather have an all-powerful smash or a spin that baffles every opponent?

46. Would you rather play pickleball on the moon with lower gravity or under the sea in an air bubble?

47. Would you rather have a paddle that honks like a clown nose every time you hit the ball or wear shoes that squeak loudly with every step?

48. Would you rather be a pickleball coach or a sports announcer for pickleball matches?

49. Would you rather always lose in the final or never make it past the first round?

50. Would you rather play wearing sunglasses or a visor?

51. Would you rather be a one-hit wonder in pickleball or a consistently good player but never a champion?

52. Would you rather always play in the morning or in the evening?

53. Would you rather have a celebrity partner in a pickleball doubles match or a pro player as your partner?

54. Would you rather be known for your sportsmanship or your skill?

55. Would you rather never make an unforced error or always be able to hit winners at will?

56. Would you rather play pickleball wearing clown makeup to every game or have to do a chicken dance every time you score a point?

57. Would you rather have a game that's strategically perfect or physically dominant?

58. Would you rather play in front of a home crowd or in an exotic location?

59. Would you rather have your matches be easy victories or challenging battles that you win?

60. Would you rather play and train in your favorite city or travel to a new city every week?

61. Would you rather have a pre-game ritual that boosts your performance or a lucky charm that you believe helps you win?

62. Would you rather have every shot you miss turn into a hilarious meme or have your victory dance go viral for its absolute lack of rhythm?

63. Would you rather always hit the perfect serve but have a weak return, or have an average serve but a killer return?

64. Would you rather be the player who makes unbelievable saves or the one who hits unreturnable shots?

65. Would you rather win all your matches but never improve, or lose often but get better each time?

66. Would you rather play in casual attire or always be decked out in the most high-end athletic wear?

67. Would you rather always play with the same partner or mix it up every tournament?

68. Would you rather be the server or the receiver in a match point situation?

69. Would you rather be known for a legendary backhand or a formidable forehand?

70. Would you rather play a championship match in pouring rain or extreme heat?

71. Would you rather be known for your defensive skills or your attacking prowess in pickleball?

72. Would you rather play a crucial game with all your sports heroes watching or have a one-on-one training session with your biggest idol?

73. Would you rather always win by a narrow margin, keeping every game exciting, or dominate and win easily every time?

74. Would you rather win a prestigious award for your sportsmanship or break a long-standing record in pickleball?

75. Would you rather be sponsored by a company that makes pickleball paddles shaped like giant pickles or a brand that makes neon, glow-in-the-dark sports attire?

APPENDIX D – 50 PICKLEBALL TRIVIA FACTS

1. When was pickleball invented?

   a) 1965
   b) 1975
   c) 1985
   d) 1995

Answer: a) 1965

2. Where was pickleball first played?

   a) Florida
   b) New York
   c) California
   d) Washington

Answer: d) Washington

3. How many players are typically on the court in a doubles pickleball game?

    a) 2
    b) 3
    c) 4
    d) 6

Answer: c) 4

4. Which of these is a fault in pickleball?

    a) Hitting the ball out of bounds
    b) Serving diagonally
    c) Playing the ball off a bounce
    d) Using an overhand serve

Answer: a) Hitting the ball out of bounds

5. What part of the court must the serve land in?

    a) The kitchen
    b) The service box
    c) Anywhere
    d) The baseline

Answer: b) The service box

6. How many points does a game of pickleball go to?

    a) 7
    b) 11
    c) 15
    d) 21

Answer: b) 11

7. How many serves do you get in pickleball?

    a) One
    b) Two
    c) Three
    d) Unlimited

Answer: a) One

8. What is the non-volley zone also known as?

    a) The kitchen
    b) The dining room
    c) The pantry
    d) The lounge

Answer: a) The kitchen

9. Which is NOT a type of pickleball paddle material?

    a) Graphite
    b) Wood

c) Steel

d) Composite

Answer: c) Steel

10. How many timeouts are allowed per team in one game?

    a) 1
    b) 2
    c) 3
    d) Unlimited

Answer: b) 2

11. How long can each timeout last?

    a) 30 seconds
    b) 1 minute
    c) 2 minutes
    d) 5 minutes

Answer: b) 1 minute

12. Which of the following is a fault?

    a) Volleying in the kitchen
    b) Serving underhand
    c) Hitting the ball after one bounce
    d) Hitting the ball out of the air

Answer: a) Volleying in the kitche

13. How many feet is the service court in length?

    a) 22 ft
    b) 44 ft
    c) 15 ft
    d) 30 ft

Answer: a) 22 ft

14. How wide is a standard pickleball court?

    a) 22 ft
    b) 20 ft
    c) 44 ft
    d) 40 ft

Answer: b) 20 ft

15, Which of the following is NOT allowed when serving in pickleball?

    a) Serving overhand
    b) Serving underhand
    c) Hitting the top of the net and landing in the correct service box
    d) Serving from the baseline

Answer: a) Serving overhand

16. How many inches above the ground should the pickleball net be at the center?

   a) 36 inches
   b) 34 inches
   c) 32 inches
   d) 38 inches

Answer: b) 34 inche

17. What's the maximum length a paddle can be?

   a) 15 inches
   b) 17 inches
   c) 19 inches
   d) 16 inches

Answer: b) 17 inche

18. If the score is even, from which side should the server serve?

   a) Right
   b) Left
   c) Any side
   d) The side opposite to the receiver

Answer: a) Right

19. What is the minimum net height at the posts?

a) 36 inches
b) 37 inches
c) 35 inches
d) 34 inches

Answer: a) 36 inches

20. What's the minimum paddle width allowed?

a) 7 inches
b) 8 inches
c) 7.5 inches
d) 9 inches

Answer: a) 7 inches

21. In which year did pickleball become a recognized sport of the National Senior Games Association?

a) 1985
b) 1995
c) 2005
d) 2015

Answer: c) 2005

22. Which of the following terms means to hit a soft shot in pickleball?

    a) Smash
    b) Drive
    c) Drop
    d) Spin

Answer: c) Drop

23. Which shot is typically used to start a point in pickleball?

    a) Smash
    b) Drive
    c) Drop
    d) Serve

Answer: d) Serve

24. In a typical game, who calls the score?

    a) The server
    b) The receiver
    c) The referee
    d) Any player on the court

Answer: a) The server

25. If a ball touches the line, is it considered in or out?

a) In

b) Out

c) It's a re-serve

d) The point is replayed

Answer: a) In

26. Which grip is commonly used in pickleball?

a) Eastern grip

b) Western grip

c) Continental grip

d) Semi-western grip

Answer: c) Continental grip

27. In which decade did the first pickleball tournament take place?

a) 1960s

b) 1970s

c) 1980s

d) 1990s

Answer: b) 1970s

28. What's the primary material of a pickleball?

    a) Rubber
    b) Plastic
    c) Leather
    d) Wood

Answer: b) Plastic

29. Which country is NOT a member of the International Federation of Pickleball?

    a) Canada
    b) India
    c) France
    d) Japan

Answer: d) Japan

30. What's the name of the space between the baseline and the no-volley line?

    a) Midline space
    b) Kitchen zone
    c) Play zone
    d) Transition zone

Answer: d) Transition zone

31. If the ball hits a player, what happens?

   a) The player's team loses the rally
   b) The player's team wins the rally
   c) The rally continues
   d) The point is replayed

Answer: a) The player's team loses the rally

32. What color is a regulation pickleball?

   a) Yellow
   b) White
   c) Green
   d) Any of the above

Answer: d) Any of the above

33. In pickleball, what term is used to describe a ball that's hit so it barely goes over the net?

   a) Lob
   b) Dink
   c) Drop
   d) Drive

Answer: b) Dink

34. Who were the original creators of pickleball?

    a) Joel Pritchard and Bill Bell
    b) John Grisham and Mike Tyson
    c) Tim Nelson and Steve Wong
    d) Roger Federer and Serena Williams

Answer: a) Joel Pritchard and Bill Bell

35. What's the goal of a third shot drop in pickleball?

    a) To end the point
    b) To transition to the net
    c) To stay at the baseline
    d) To defend against a smash

Answer: b) To transition to the net

36. How many points does a team need to win by to secure a game?

    a) 1
    b) 2
    c) 3
    d) 4

Answer: b) 2

37. If a player's foot is on the no-volley line during a volley, what happens?

  a) They receive a warning
  b) It's considered a fault
  c) Play continues as normal
  d) They lose a serve

Answer: b) It's considered a fault

38. Which shot is typically used to keep the opponent at the baseline?

  a) Lob
  b) Dink
  c) Drop
  d) Drive

Answer: d) Drive

39. How is the double bounce rule applied in pickleball?

  a) Both teams must let the ball bounce once before volleying
  b) The ball can bounce twice in a rally
  c) Only the serving team must let the ball bounce once
  d) Only the receiving team must let the ball bounce twice

Answer: a) Both teams must let the ball bounce once before volleying

40. What's the maximum thickness of a pickleball paddle?

    a) 1 inch
    b) 2 inches
    c) 3 inches
    d) There's no maximum thickness

Answer: d) There's no maximum thickness

41. In which city was the first official pickleball tournament held?

    a) Seattle
    b) New York
    c) Miami
    d) Los Angeles

Answer: a) Seattle

42. When was the USA Pickleball Association (USAPA) established?

    a) 1967
    b) 1972
    c) 1984
    d) 2005

Answer: c) 1984

43. What's a "poach" in pickleball?

  a) A type of serve
  b) A shot played in the air
  c) Crossing into a partner's area to play a ball
  d) A spinning shot

Answer: c) Crossing into a partner's area to play a ball

44. What is the initial bounce in the double bounce rule referred to as?

  a) First bounce
  b) Double hit
  c) Service bounce
  d) Drop bounce

Answer: a) First bounce

45. How many seconds does the server have to serve after calling the score?

  a) 5 seconds
  b) 10 seconds
  c) 15 seconds
  d) There's no time limit

Answer: b) 10 seconds

46. Which state in the USA has the most pickleball courts?

   a) Florida
   b) California
   c) Arizona
   d) Washington

Answer: a) Florida

47. When playing doubles, who serves first from the receiving team after a side out?

   a) The player on the left
   b) The player on the right
   c) The player who did not serve last
   d) The player who received the last serve

Answer: b) The player on the right

48. What is the term for hitting the ball in a manner that it spins differently than expected?

   a) Smash
   b) Slice
   c) Dink
   d) Spin

Answer: b) Slice

49. In a game to 11, when do teams typically switch sides?

a) After 5 points
b) After 6 points
c) After 10 points
d) They don't switch sides

Answer: b) After 6 points

50. Which term describes a ball that is hit with top-spin in pickleball?

a) Lob
b) Drive
c) Roll
d) Push

Answer: c) Roll

APPENDIX E – 50 FUN FAMILY TEAM NAMES

- The Pickleball Rockets
- Smashin' Paddles
- Dink Dynasty
- Volley Llamas
- The Overhanders
- Doubles Trouble
- Servin' Up Aces
- The Backhand Bandits
- Net Ninjas
- Pickleball Maniacs
- Paddle Whackers
- The Volley Monsters
- Ace's Angels
- The Slamma Jammas
- Cobra Kai Pickleball Dojo
- The Fantastic Paddlers

- Sweet Pickleball Feet
- Los Picklebolos Magnificos
- The Points Pointers
- Rally Rascals
- The Pickleball Fanatics
- Paddle Pandemonium
- Court Jesters
- Dinkin' Dunkin Pickles
- Net Gainers
- Ace of Smash
- Bump, Set, Pickle
- Pickleball Mania
- Paddle Whack Attack
- The Rim Rockers
- Pickleball Gang
- Smashing Dills
- Mad Dog Dinkers
- Rally Cats
- Pickleball Lords
- Grand Slam Fam
- Sweet Pickles
- Dill With It
- Cannon Smashers
- The Pop N Lobs
- The Pickleball Clan
- Paddle Powerhouse
- The Smashin' Siblings
- Volley Vanguard
- The Net Knights

- Ace Avengers
- Family Ralliers
- Pickleball Fusion
- The Spin Doctors
- The Dink Dominators

APPENDIX F – 50 SONGS FOR YOUR FAMILY'S PICKLEBALL PLAYLIST

Pickleball

1. The Pickleball Song – Holderness Family Music [1] -
2. Pickleball Symphony – Holderness Family Music [2]
3. Ode to Pickleball - "Wrecking Ball" Parody – Holderness Family Music [3]
4. If Pearl Jam Explained Pickleball Rules – Holderness Family Music[4]
5. "I'm Gonna Be (500 Miles)" - The Proclaimers: An upbeat tempo pairs well with pickleball's active pace.

6. "Good Vibrations" - The Beach Boys: Sets a positive and feel-good atmosphere for sports.

7. "Jump Around" - House of Pain: Provides high energy and is perfect for celebrating victories.

8. "Lean On Me" - Bill Withers: Reflects the importance of teamwork and support in sports.

9. "Walking on Sunshine" - Katrina & The Waves: Captures the fun and lighthearted spirit of pickleball.

10. "Don't Stop Me Now" - Queen: Fast-paced and motivating, ideal for competitive games.

11. "Stand By Me" - Ben E. King: Encourages unity and standing by teammates during tough points.

12. "Shake It Off" - Taylor Swift: Helps players shrug off mistakes and stay focused on the game.

13. "Happy" - Pharrell Williams: Uplifting and spreads joy on the courts, enhancing the playing experience.

14. "We Are Family" - Sister Sledge: Fosters camaraderie and team bonding, crucial in sports.

15. "Can't Stop the Feeling" - Justin Timberlake: An upbeat, feel-good song perfect for getting pumped up to play.

16. "Good Time" - Owl City & Carly Rae Jepsen: High energy and fun, aligns with the lively nature of sports.

17. "I Gotta Feeling" - Black Eyed Peas: A celebratory song for victorious moments on the court.

18. "Let's Groove" - Earth, Wind & Fire: A smooth, danceable track that keeps players moving around the court.

19. "24K Magic" - Bruno Mars: Funky and fast-paced, providing an energetic boost during play.

20. "Footloose" - Kenny Loggins: Encourages players to shake off nerves and move freely on the court.

21. "Girls Just Want to Have Fun" - Cyndi Lauper: An anthem about enjoying oneself, perfect for sports.

22. "The Middle" - Zedd, Maren Morris & Grey: An upbeat and rallying cry for overcoming challenges in the game.

23. "Dynamite" - BTS: A fun and pump-up song with explosive energy, keeping players motivated.

24. "Who Let the Dogs Out" - Baha Men: A lively and spirited song that lifts players' spirits.

25. "Celebration" - Kool & the Gang: A jubilant song that fits perfectly for celebrating victories in sports.

26. "Eye of the Tiger" - Survivor: A classic motivational song that ignites the competitive spirit.

27. "Shape of You" - Ed Sheeran: A catchy and rhythmic tune that complements the game's tempo.

28. "Uptown Funk" - Mark Ronson ft. Bruno Mars: Sets the tone for groove and rhythm during play.

29. "Livin' on a Prayer" - Bon Jovi: High-energy rock to keep players moving and motivated.

30. "Shut Up and Dance" - Walk the Moon: A fun and danceable track that encourages players to let loose.

31. "Jump" - Van Halen: A classic rock anthem that fuels players with excitement and energy.

32. "All Star" - Smash Mouth: Energetic and upbeat, perfectly aligning with the spirit of sports.

33. "Dance Monkey" - Tones and I: A catchy and playful tune that adds enjoyment to the game.

34. "Sweet Caroline" - Neil Diamond: A sing-along classic that enhances the fun atmosphere of sports.

35. "Born to Run" - Bruce Springsteen: Encouraging and exhilarating, motivating players to give their best.

36. "Livin' La Vida Loca" - Ricky Martin: Infuses Latin-inspired energy into the game.

37. "Don't Stop 'Til You Get Enough" - Michael Jackson: A timeless dance hit that keeps players moving.

38. "Sugar" - Maroon 5: Sweet and lively, contributing to the overall enjoyment of the game.

39. "Shake Your Body (Down to the Ground)" - The Jacksons: A dance-floor filler that adds rhythm and movement.

40. "Footloose" - Kenny Loggins: Ideal for active moments on the court, encouraging players to move freely.

41. "Billie Jean" - Michael Jackson: Classic with a killer bassline that complements the game's intensity.

42. "I Gotta Feeling" - The Black Eyed Peas: A party anthem perfect for celebrating victories in sports.

43. "Dare" - Gorillaz: Energetic and electronic, providing a dynamic background for play.

44. "Dynamite" - BTS: An explosive track that keeps players moving and motivated.

45. "September" - Earth, Wind & Fire: Funky and soulful, adding a touch of groove to the game.

46. "Rock Your Body" - Justin Timberlake: Irresistible rhythm that keeps players in sync with the game.

47. "Superstition" - Stevie Wonder: Funky and groovy, enhancing the enjoyment of sports.

48. "Party Rock Anthem" - LMFAO: A party-starting hit that brings a lively atmosphere to the game.

49. "Stronger" - Kanye West: Motivating and dynamic, encouraging players to give their all.

50. "Firework" - Katy Perry: Uplifting and empowering, inspiring players to shine on the court.

NOTES

1. THE HISTORY & APPEAL OF PICKLEBALL

1. Sports & Fitness Industry Association (SFIA). "2023 Pickleball Single Report."
2. International Pickleball Federation. "About the International Pickleball Federation." Accessed August 2023. https://theipf.org/about.html.
3. Holderness Family. "The 5 Stages of Pickleball." YouTube Video. Accessed July 2023. https://youtu.be/tYX5l6js01U?si=29iikvl7hPvYO6x7.
4. "2023 Juniors US Pickleball Open Gold Medal Match U14." YouTube Video. Accessed September 2023. https://youtu.be/3E5L4U0gpDs?si=BG6ppUwEy-W3nbuzE.
5. "2023 Junior Girls US Pickleball Open Gold Medal Match U14." YouTube Video. Accessed September 2023. https://youtu.be/WSZKmD-oeOY?si=jwNXFK0ASs94U3qQ.
6. That YouTub3 Family - The Adventurers. "Pickleball Battle – Losers do Chores!" YouTube Video. Accessed September 2023. https://www.youtube.com/watch?v=yPrvGoHqSB0.
7. Gates, Bill. "Fifty years ago, I started playing this little-known sport with a funny name. Now, it's all the rage." GateNotes. Blog post, July 26, 2022.

2. GEARING UP – EQUIPMENT ESSENTIALS

1. "Paddle Guide." Pickleball Central. Accessed August 2023. https://www.pickleballcentral.com.
2. Ben Johns. "What's in My Bag." YouTube Video. Accessed July 2023. https://www.youtube.com/watch?v=-I_I5fK0QgU
3. "Athlete Anna Leigh Waters." Accessed July 2023. http://www.ppatour.com/athlete/anna-leigh-waters/.

3. THE PICKLEBALL BASICS – KNOW THE COURT AND GRASP THE GROUND RULES

1. Better Pickleball. "Pickleball Scoring Basics – Make it Easy with Me, You and Who?" YouTube Video. Accessed July 2023. https://youtu.be/eMEpFip-Idrk?si=edZl4nR1wIC-ZUgO.

2. "Double Bounce Rule Explained." Video by Better Pickleball. Accessed July 2023. https://youtu.be/ItNAehNnO8g?si=N4w6nCQzKHYOfOBr.

3. Pickleball Channel. "Non-Volley Rule Explained." Accessed July 2023. https://www.pickleballchannel.com/PB411-NVZ-Rule.

4. Pickleball Channel. "The Underhand Serve." Accessed July 2023. https://www.pickleballchannel.com/pickleball-411-the-underhand-serve/.

5. Pickleball Guy, The. How to Serve: A Beginner's Guide. YouTube Video. Accessed September 2023. https://youtu.be/BmdnJNCEwxI?si=m2Mw-FY5W_nVHCjmL.

6. Guinness World Records. "Longest Pickleball Rally." Accessed September 2023. https://www.guinnessworldrecords.com/world-records/669898-longest-pickleball-rally.

7. The Pickleball Guy. "7 Kitchen Strategies to Avoid Getting Crushed in Pickleball." YouTube Video. Accessed July 2023. https://youtu.be/JxVFdb1PixU?si=-XHkzNPVRSUwUAt9.

8. "Pickleball Channel." 5 Steps to a Winning Dink. Video. Accessed July 2023. https://www.pickleballchannel.com/PB411-Dinking-101.

9. Kim Kardashian Plays Pickleball. Facebook Video. Accessed July 2023. https://fb.watch/nuBvG1tP9f/.

4. BEGINNER'S STRATEGIES FOR SUCCESS

1. PrimeTime Pickleball. Deep Serves and Returns. YouTube Video. Accessed September 2023. https://www.youtube.com/watch?v=nKQU52FB_2s.

2. PrimeTime Pickleball. Slow Motion Serves with Top Players. YouTube Video. Accessed September 2023. https://youtu.be/egBPPooOBVQ?si=88YOavDFpVlmdj_5.

3. "Pickleball Channel." Three Serves and Why You Need Them. YouTube Video. Accessed July 2023. https://www.pickleballchannel.com/pickleball-411-three-serves-and-why-you-need-them/.

4. Pickleball Magazine. Pickleball Quick Tip: How to Hit a Better Return of Serve. YouTube Video. Accessed July 2023. https://youtu.be/cX-nyshUCQQ?

si=_vJKhEdhMxPDooq6.

5. Pickleball Guy, The. 3rd Shot Drop vs. Drive: Which to use and WHEN? YouTube Video. Accessed September 2023. https://youtu.be/LnTAm5pAr9c?si=oUGyob6S1yW77mqY.

6. Cincola, John. Court Positioning Fundamentals: You Can't Play Great Pickleball Unless You're in the Right Spot. YouTube Video. Accessed September 2023. https://youtu.be/5R60Yi7nUt8?si=FRXAyKAxs7CXG4OB.

7. Pickleball Guy, The. 6 Pickleball Doubles Strategies New Players MUST Know. YouTube Video. Accessed September 2023. https://www.youtube.com/watch?v=JGMLn68RZS8.

8. Professional Pickleball Association Tour. "Ben Johns." Accessed July 2023. http://www.ppatour.com/athlete/ben-johns/.

5. PRACTICE MAKES PERFECT – DRILLS TO ELEVATE YOUR PICKLEBALL GAME

1. ESPN. "Kevin Durant latest sports star to own pickleball franchise." Accessed September 2023. https://www.espn.com/nba/story/_/id/34838548/kevin-durant-latest-sports-star-own-pickleball-franchise.

6. OVERCOMING OBSTACLES: TACKLING TRICKY SERVES AND MORE

1. Selkirk Sport. "Pickleball, Parkinson's, and Persistence: The Inspiring Journey of Scott Rider." Accessed September 2023. https://www.selkirk.com/blogs/spotlights/pickleball-parkinsons-and-persistence-the-inspiring-journey-of-scott-rider.

2. Johns, Ben. The Keys to Gaining Mental Strength on the Pickleball Court. YouTube Video. Accessed September 2023. https://youtu.be/oCvDxodJESQ?si=cMKlcMI47EwI34hO.

3. Pickleball Union. "Meet Peruvian Miranda Cabieses: Pickleball Winner, Ambassador, and Fundraiser." Accessed October 2023. https://pickleballunion.com/meet-peruvian-miranda-cabieses-pickleball-winner-ambassador-and-fundraiser/.

8. THE PICKLEBALL COMMUNITY: YOUR NEW HOME AWAY FROM HOME

1. Chronicles_of_IMan. Instagram profile. Accessed September 2023. https://www.instagram.com/Chronicles_of_IMan.

9. THE GENTLE(WO)MAN'S GAME – ETIQUETTE AND FAIR PLAY IN PICKLEBALL

1. Pickleball Magazine. "'Hurricane' Tyra Black Takes Pickleball by Storm." Accessed October 2023. https://www.pickleballmagazine.com/cover-story-2/%E2%80%98hurricane%E2%80%99-tyra-black-takes-pickleball-by-storm.

10. VENTURING INTO COMPETITIVE PLAY – THE FAMILY EDITION

1. USA Pickleball. "USA Pickleball Official Rulebook 2023 v4.1." 2023. Accessed October 2023. https://usapickleball.org/docs/USA-Pickleball-Official-Rulebook-2023-v4-1.pdf.
2. Major League Pickleball. "Hayden Patriquin." Accessed October 2023. https://www.majorleaguepickleball.net/player/hayden-patriquin/.

APPENDIX A – WHO'S WHO OF PICKLEBALL

1. Major League Pickleball. "Premier League." Accessed October 2023. https://www.majorleaguepickleball.net/premier-league/.

APPENDIX F – 50 SONGS FOR YOUR FAMILY'S PICKLEBALL PLAYLIST

1. Holderness Family Music. The Pickleball Song. YouTube Video. Accessed October 2023. https://www.youtube.com/watch?v=MtEWJSc_FJw.

2. Holderness Family Music. Pickleball Symphony. YouTube Video. Accessed October 2023. https://www.youtube.com/watch?v=oQhPA9irWPk.

3. Holderness Family Music. Ode to Pickleball - "Wrecking Ball" Parody. YouTube Video. Accessed October 2023. https://www.youtube.com/watch?v=95_HeEELzYU.

4. Holderness Family Music. If Pearl Jam Explained Pickleball Rules. YouTube Video. Accessed October 2023. https://youtube.com/shorts/iHDq53ZqBzk?si=fJGlkaan_ryoS9Xk.

Made in the USA
Columbia, SC
18 July 2024

38821864R00127